Assessing the Needs of Bilingual Pupils

Living in Two Languages

Second Edition

By Deryn Hall

revised and updated by

**Dominic Griffiths, Liz Haslam
and Yvonne Wilkin**

David Fulton Publishers
London

David Fulton Publishers Ltd
Ormond House, 26–27 Boswell Street, London WC1N 3JZ

www.fultonpublishers.co.uk

First published in Great Britain by David Fulton Publishers Ltd 1995. Reprinted 1995, 1996, 1997, 1998, 1999
Second edition 2001

British Library Cataloguing in Publication Data
A catalogue record for this book is available from the British Library.

ISBN 1-85346-799-5

The publishers would like to thank Lyn Corson for copy-editing and Ray Jarman for proofreading this book.

Typeset by Textype Typesetters, Cambridge
Printed in Great Britain by Bell and Bain Ltd, Glasgow

Contents

Acknowledgements

This book was produced as part of my work for the London Borough of Tower Hamlets in helping schools with the identification and assessment of bilingual pupils causing learning concern. I have been fortunate to work alongside colleagues from the Language Support Service, the Educational Psychology Service and the Support for Learning Service as well as many teachers from mainstream primary and secondary schools who have provided a sounding board for the ideas included here.

I am particularly indebted to John Hutchings, Principal Educational Psychologist, Tower Hamlets for pointing me in the right direction and for alerting me to some of the pioneering work done in this field via articles in the *Information Exchange for Educational Psychologists*. These were edited and published by John from 1985 to 1989 in the days of the Inner London Education Authority.

Thanks also go to my colleagues in the Language Support central team, the local schools where I have worked and to the bilingual children of London's East End for providing me with a constant source of challenge, material and inspiration for this handbook.

Deryn Hall

Preface to the first edition

This handbook is offered as a guide to all teachers working in multilingual and multicultural schools.

Together with some background information, it offers some practical ways of raising and considering the issues involved in the assessment of bilingual pupils whose learning is causing concern. Unfortunately there are no magic answers, no simple tests or instant solutions. However, I remain convinced that teachers and schools have within their power the means that will lead to a greater awareness and more accurate assessment of the needs of these pupils.

There may be a wide variety of reasons why a bilingual child is not learning successfully at school and these will need to be fully considered before assumptions of learning difficulty are made.

The Code of Practice (Department for Education (DfE) 1994) now sets a clear expectation that the school will actively seek parents' (and older pupils' own) views where learning difficulties are registered. The expertise of language support staff, bilingual staff, community advice and interpreters/translators may also enhance early identification and assessment of special educational needs (SEN).

The main concern for teachers of bilingual pupils learning in a second language is how to separate temporary issues of language acquisition from longer term learning difficulties. It is in response to these voiced concerns that this handbook is offered.

Deryn Hall
Tower Hamlets 1995

Preface to the second edition

Since its publication in 1995, the first edition of this handbook has been of enormous help to countless teachers, other professionals and learners in the numerous contexts of bilingual education.

Significant developments in education and educational legislation over the last decade have necessitated an update of the text to reflect the issues and currents of thought that characterise pedagogy today.

The second edition therefore reflects the changes envisaged in the Revised Draft Code of Practice on the Identification and Assessment of Special Educational Needs (Department for Education and Employment (DfEE) 2000a), the publication of step descriptors for language proficiency by the Qualifications and Curriculum Authority (QCA) as well as recent legislation and changes in organisation for staff teaching English as an Additional Language (EAL), and examines their implications for the assessment of the needs of bilingual learners.

It was a pleasure for us to be involved in bringing the second edition up to date for 2001. The collaboration between Ethnic Minority Achievement Grant (EMAG)-funded and SEN staff presented valuable opportunities for cross-fertilisation of ideas and practices in the shared context of inclusive education.

Dominic Griffiths, Liz Haslam, Yvonne Wilkin
Tameside 2001

1 Introduction

There has long been an unacknowledged relationship between bilingualism and special education as evidenced by the disproportionate numbers of immigrant and minority language children 'deported' into special education classes ... in many countries.

(Cummins 1984)

Handicapping conditions do not respect ethnic, geographical, religious or any other boundaries imposed by man.

(Miller 1984)

Acknowledging our pluralistic society

Much educational literature is still produced without any reference to the fact that Britain is increasingly a multicultural and multilingual society. There is little excuse for this as it can no longer be seen as merely an issue for inner city schools. Linguistic diversity is now a norm in British classrooms. Most teachers across the country can expect to have some experience of pupils whose first language is other than English. Because, on the whole, schools continue to reflect the middle-class monocultural, monolingual values of a majority society, pupils' academic potential (or IQ) is still assessed in relation to these norms. Fortunately, larger numbers of minority language pupils, and a concern for educational inclusion to ensure equality of opportunity, have caused educators to re-examine some of these assessment practices and to acknowledge that they may be inappropriate for an increasing number of pupils.

Any assessment of bilingual pupils' learning progress needs to ascertain whether a pupil has a learning disability or is merely experiencing a temporary language barrier as a result of insufficient exposure to English. Unfortunately this assessment is no simple matter, and there is no single language and culture bias-free test that can provide ready-made answers. Rather, the issue begs a wide range of further questions. What is the nature of learning ability and disability? What are the principles of language acquisition? What is the relationship between first and second language skills? How long does it take to acquire English proficiency and what do we mean by that? What are the differences between social and academic fluency?

These questions and issues cause monolingual teachers and educational psychologists (EPs) considerable anxiety when the educational progress of a bilingual child is giving concern. This handbook suggests that the information gained will only

1

be as good as the questions asked, the information/evidence of learning gathered and the teaching provision/intervention made. These issues are further explored in Chapters 4, 5 and 6.

Separating issues of 'language' from 'learning'

Since litigation in the USA during the late 1960s and early 1970s, educators have been at pains to spell out the necessity of distinguishing between second language barriers and learning difficulties that may account for an individual bilingual pupil's failure to make learning progress. A landmark case (*Diana* v. *State Board of Education*, California 1970) established rights to a non-biased assessment for ethnic minority pupils, so that, in the 1981 Education Act (Department of Education and Science (DES) 1981) which served to define SEN for England and Wales, the following clear statement appeared:

> A child is not to be taken as having a learning difficulty solely because the language (or form of language) in which he is, or will be, taught is different from a language (or form of language) which has at any time been spoken in his home.

It is important that the provision made for EAL is not confused with SEN remediation. This was underlined in the 1993 Education Act (DfE 1993). It is a sad reflection of today's schools that some teachers still equate a lack of English language skills with learning problems and low intelligence.

Some pupils learning through EAL will need support to extend their speaking and writing repertoires and to practise new words and phrases in a relevant context. They will need to acquire sufficient linguistic competence in order that their understanding of processes and concepts is fully developed. An Office for Standards in Education (OFSTED) paper describes some of the most effective lessons as those that 'included the use of specially prepared materials to match the pupils' levels of English and educational experience, and tasks which enabled them to work purposefully with their peers and encouraged them to become increasingly independent of support' (OFSTED 1994b).

Pupils with SEN, on the other hand, may require specific targeted support for their individual learning difficulty (this may also involve support for a specific disability or for emotional/behavioural difficulty). The guidance issued in the Revised Draft Code of Practice (DfEE 2000a) suggests that such identified pupils should be formally registered on a SEN 'stage of concern' by the school and their progress regularly monitored in consultation with parents and in partnership with other professionals. At the stages of School Action and School Action Plus this will involve drawing up an Individual Education Plan (IEP) (see Chapter 6).

However, both groups of pupils require support in order to gain full access to the curriculum to which they have entitlement. To some extent, it could be argued that what is good practice for one group is also good practice for the other, as the necessary degree of curriculum differentiation, thought and planning evidenced in successful lessons would inevitably improve the learning of all pupils. One such example of integrated good practice is described in 'a school with a multidisciplinary team approach (SEN, home/school liaison and specialist EAL staff) to meet the learning needs of individual pupils. Careful planning and systematic record keeping ensured that only one additional teacher participated in any one lesson but that all teachers worked to the agreed programme of support' (OFSTED 1994b).

However, distinction must be clearly made between the individual learning needs of bilingual pupils and pupils with SEN, and different appropriate provision needs to be offered. Schools must ensure that lack of English proficiency is not assumed to indicate SEN or learning difficulties.

Notwithstanding, a percentage of bilingual pupils is likely to experience SEN at some point of their school life and there is no hard evidence to suggest that this is either more or less than we might expect to find in the monolingual population. As this is reckoned nationally to be around 20 per cent of the school population, we can expect a proportionate and representative spread of bilingual pupils to be at each SEN stage at any given time. This is a fairly crude figure but is a simple measure that a school can use as an indicator of the understanding of the issues involved within their institution, where the numbers of pupils learning through EAL are large enough to form a representative sample.

A language approach to the curriculum

It is now universally agreed that language in its broadest sense of communicative competence is central to the learning process in the acquisition of a second language. It was previously believed that bilingual pupils learning English needed different teaching methods and materials that were somehow separate from those relevant or appropriate to other pupils. Linguists and educationalists have recognised that the teaching methodologies developed as a response to mixed ability classes are also those that are relevant and appropriate for bilingual learners (e.g. Cummins 1996). Developments in matching teaching approaches to a wider range of learning styles present interesting opportunities in this area (see Riding and Rayner 1998). The slow recognition of the growing linguistic diversity of mainstream classrooms has reinforced the need to find inclusive teaching methods and materials.

It has also become clear that exclusive methodologies could threaten equality of opportunity and be seen as racially divisive. As a direct result of the findings of Swann (Department of Education and Science (DES) 1985) and the Calderdale investigation (Commission for Racial Equality (CRE) 1986), separate off-site withdrawal units for pupils new to English were deemed as clearly discriminatory on social, linguistic and educational grounds. It is now standard practice in this country to try to support pupils learning through EAL within the mainstream classroom as part of normal lessons. Furthermore, there is considerable interest from some other European countries who are looking at the best of this inclusive practice in Britain as a model of how to educate their own recent refugee or immigrant populations.

Encouraging skills and versatility in speaking and listening is vital in developing understanding of ideas and experiences. The metacognitive processes of thinking out loud, formulating thought and talking through ideas are an essential part of the learning process. Pupils who engage orally in the language of a subject with their peers are more likely to understand and internalise the related concepts. Language teachers, working in partnership with mainstream curriculum colleagues to plan collaborative group activities, can help to provide learning materials in which contextual clues ensure fuller access to tasks for all pupils. (Many practising teachers using this methodology swap their teaching materials through membership of the Collaborative Learning Project – see Useful addresses.) These materials allow bilingual pupils, as well as those with learning difficulties, more chance of working on their understanding at an appropriate cognitive level of challenge than materials that are reliant on decoding skills alone. Typical exchanges during oral collaborative tasks might include practising language structures such as questioning, reflecting, suggesting, prediction and forming hypotheses.

For some bilingual pupils, the opportunity to use a language other than English to support learning and understanding in the classroom will provide a way of enhancing the conceptualisation of complex ideas and confirm language and meaning. Bilingual pupils, particularly those from minority immigrant or refugee groups, need support to gain good academic qualifications without which their employment prospects will be drastically reduced. This should not be at the expense of their first language skills however, as their facility and literacy in dual languages is also a marketable commodity.

2 Bilingual pupils

A working definition

There have been many attempts to define bilingualism during the past 50 years ranging from earlier narrow definitions to the broader ones of Skutnabb-Kangas (1981). The one used in this book, and from which it takes its subtitle, is the working definition adopted by the London Borough of Tower Hamlets (Shell 1992):

> Bilingual: In England the term is currently used to refer to pupils who live in two languages, who have access to, or need to use, two or more languages at home and at school. It does not mean that they have fluency in both languages or that they are competent and literate in both languages.

Different groups of bilingual children

Teachers cannot assume that all bilingual children they may come across in schools are one homogeneous group. There are likely to be differing pressures, depending on the context in which the pupils need to acquire the new language, that will determine the pupils' investment in learning. Bilingual pupils fall roughly into the following categories.

Elite bilinguals

These are the children of those families who travel abroad from choice, usually for business, academic or diplomatic reasons. They are often children of upper/middle-class professionals whose first language is in no way threatened and which is maintained at home and by visits to their home country. For these children, bilingualism is viewed as enriching and they are unlikely to become educationally disadvantaged even if they do not achieve full fluency in their second language.

Linguistic majorities

This group of pupils are those from a large group where they are learning a second language either because the schools offer a more prestigious minority/or world language (e.g. English in Hong Kong), or offer an immersion programme such as French immersion in Canada.

Bilingual families

Some children will come from homes where a different language is spoken by one parent. If this is a minority language then there is no external pressure to become bilingual even though there may well be family, cultural or religious pressure, e.g. from grandparents.

Linguistic minorities

This is likely to be the group of most concern to teachers. Whether they are from refugee, immigrant or minority group families, the home language is likely to have a low status or value in the new society. Children from these families will be subjected to strong pressure to learn the language of the majority community and will need to become competent in speaking, reading and writing for economic survival. They are also likely to be under pressure from their families not only to take advantage of better educational opportunities but also to retain their first language and culture. For the children from many Bangladeshi communities, for example, this often means learning standard Bengali and mosque Arabic, as well as learning English at school and retaining the spoken home language of Sylheti.

What the research tells us

The following list is a summary of the most important points to emerge from the extensive research into the acquisition of second language (Cummins 1984; Dulay *et al.* 1982; Desforges and Kerr 1984; Skutnabb-Kangas 1981) (see photocopiable sheet on p. 78). They are well substantiated and should be adopted by teachers as basic premises.

- Children take up to two years to develop 'basic interpersonal communication skills' (playground/street survival language) BUT it takes much longer, perhaps up to seven years or more, to acquire the full range of literacy skills ('cognitive academic language proficiency') needed to cope with the literacy demands of GCSE.
- A silent (receptive) period is natural for some pupils when learning a second language and not a sign of learning difficulties in the first/early stages.
- There are developmental factors common to both native and additional language acquisition. For more information, refer to Cummins (1996) and the 'dual iceberg' theory.
- Teachers/schools should have basic information available about the language backgrounds of bilingual pupils (see Chapter 4).
- There should be an awareness by all that a focus on the first language is a valuable channel to support learning and NOT a hindrance. Teachers should not advocate the use of English only, either at school or at home.
- Parents should be encouraged to share language and literacy in speaking and listening as well as in reading and writing. This can be as valuable in first/home language as in English.

- Bilingualism can be educationally enriching and has a positive effect on intellectual performance.
- Bilingualism should be valued as a special achievement.
- Where there are academic difficulties, teachers should first critically examine the teaching they are offering in terms of motivation and language use.

Good practice in teaching bilingual pupils

There is a wide consensus in this country as to what constitutes good practice in the teaching of bilingual children in the mainstream classroom. The view now is that the education of bilingual pupils is the responsibility of all teachers and not simply that of EAL or specially funded support staff where these are available. The methodologies of partnership teaching, active teaching and learning, collaborative and group work, and the role of oracy in classrooms all contribute to a body of knowledge about good practice which has a particular relevance for bilingual pupils (see the practical ideas for language work in schools in Shell 1992; Buxton 1994; Cummins 1996).

Partnership teaching

One of the arguments for the promotion of partnership teaching (Bourne and McPake 1991) emphasises changing practice to take account of the diversity of both language and learning needs within the classroom. The curriculum offered must be accessible and relevant to all pupils' needs and teachers should evaluate their practice in meeting these needs accordingly.

Partnership teaching, as described in Bourne and McPake (1991), is a broader model than that of one class or subject teacher working together with one language support teacher inside a classroom. It requires a commitment from the senior management of the school to a model of shared planning, and the expertise of pairs or groups of teachers and other partners working together to access curriculum both inside and outside the classroom. The organisation of the classroom to enable pupils to work in groups and the benefit of this for bilingual pupils cannot be emphasised enough. This is now more feasible than ever with the expansion of the use of support assistants in the mainstream classroom.

Oracy: the role of talk in classrooms

Talk is a vital key to language acquisition and the active learning strategies encouraged by the National Oracy Project (1987–1993) demonstrated the benefit of talk in the learning process. Encouraging skills and versatility in speaking and listening is vital in developing understanding of ideas and experiences. Pupils are expected to produce written outcomes as evidence of learning in our examination systems. Yet speech is the primary instrument of thought and argument. Expressive narrative, story telling and writing are important links in learning to the production of transactional formal prose. Douglas Barnes (1992) aptly describes the role of talk in classrooms as a way of 'working on understanding'. It is no accident that OFSTED inspectors are asked to comment on oracy, equated with literacy and numeracy, across the curriculum. Pupils encouraged to express themselves orally are also ultimately more likely to have a voice in democratic society.

Use of first language in classrooms

For bilingual pupils, the opportunity to use their first language at school is a way of confirming language and meaning to support learning. Many bilingual pupils come from cultures with a strong oral tradition. For example, the Somali language had no written form until 1972 and all religious, academic and cultural learning was handed down orally. These oral literacy traditions, which are vital to the well-being of a culture, rely on very advanced skills of memory, speaking and listening; we should capitalise on these and acknowledge that some will need fostering and reviving.

Pupils must be encouraged to use their first languages in the classroom, but they will be more prepared to support their learning and understanding in this way if their community language is given a high status at school. For this reason, pupils' home languages and experiences must not only be valued and recognised in school but also developed and utilised. Parents also frequently need help and reassurance to recognise the vital role that sustaining and developing oracy and literacy in the home language can play in learning. Research suggests that facility in a first language is a help rather than a hindrance to learning in a second language. Sadly, children whose own first language is not well established by school age are statistically likely to be at a severe disadvantage in acquiring a second language, as the underlying conceptual and linguistic proficiency will not be sufficiently developed to aid transfer (Cummins 1984).

Active and collaborative learning in small groups

Pupils working cooperatively on tasks in groups share skills and support each other. This method of delivering the curriculum emphasises and actively encourages oral work that helps to formulate and expand ideas. During the problem-solving process, pupils use skills of negotiating, prioritising, investigating, drafting, sequencing and matching.

Using active learning strategies in the classroom frees teachers from the traditional role of instructor for some of the time. This enables them to spend more time with small groups, or SEN pupils needing additional support, as the class is organised to work on tasks in groups. It also engenders a sense of personal involvement, self-esteem and ownership among pupils – all important factors in empowering them to take responsibility for their own learning. The talk engendered by the group process maximises opportunities for bilingual pupils to order, classify and transform information and to experience, test, shape and interpret meaning. How groups are organised can be a vital element in their success. Pupils new to English need to be grouped with supportive peers, particularly if there is a shared first language. However, it is not good practice to group all first-language speakers together as groups need to include good pupil models of English. Many proven models of group organisation, balance and change are provided by Reid *et al.* (1989) and Cummins (1996).

The identification and assessment of pupils causing concern

What is it?

Before funding of EAL teachers switched to the DfEE, the Home Office clearly requested that Section 11-funded project teachers should monitor targeted bilingual students using language levels or stages. Many local education authorities (LEAs) based their models on the work of Hilary Hester (Barrs *et al.* 1990). Using variations of her published language stages (which are descriptions of language behaviour in its broadest communicative sense), teachers have assessed and plotted the progress of bilingual pupils. Interpreting these has led to much local discussion and the need for moderation in many LEAs. A consensus as to what evidence at each stage is looked for across the four language skills of listening, speaking, reading and writing has been developed in many parts of the country (see Chapter 5).

Teachers and departments who have been involved in supporting bilingual learners in schools have built up considerable knowledge and expertise in normative (related to their school population and locality) expected rates and patterns of progress in the acquisition of English. Often they have considerable understanding of patterns of typical errors made by particular linguistic groups, which relate to the differences and structures in the first language (see Chapter 5).

Where there is informed concern about lack of progress in learning across time, the question must be raised as to whether the pupil should be registered under the Revised Draft Code of Practice (DfEE 2000a) as having SEN.

Although some bilingual pupils are likely to experience SEN in much the same way as the indigenous population, these pupils need to be clearly distinguished from those in the early stages of acquiring English (see Chapter 7).

Why should we do it?

Teachers are required to assess pupils' learning progress as part of the normal cycle of planning, teaching and assessing. If second language acquisition is confused with cognitive learning difficulties, or cultural adjustment with social adjustment and behaviour difficulties, we risk falling into the trap of falsely labelling and inappropriately educating young people who will either underachieve or suffer entrenched difficulties as a result of being falsely identified. Such mistakes were made in the past and we need to work with more sensitivity and increased awareness in the light of the greater knowledge and experience available to us.

There may be many reasons why a bilingual pupil is not learning successfully at school and all of these possible causes must be considered before a child is 'registered' as having SEN.

How to do it

At the end of Chapter 3 a model or 'map' for the process of identifying and assessing bilingual pupils causing concern is introduced. By following subsequent chapters you will have a range of practical ideas that you can copy or adapt for use in your school.

3 The identification and assessment of bilingual pupils causing concern

The process of learning a language should not be equated with SEN. This principle has important implications for planning. For example, the placing of EAL pupils within groups, enabling them to draw on prior experience, and providing them with scaffolded English Language support, should help them to engage with the curriculum at the appropriate cognitive level.

(National Association for Language Development in the Curriculum (NALDIC) 1999)

The issues involved

Where there is concern about a child's educational progress, it is vital that teachers distinguish between issues of lack of English language acquisition and those of learning. The collection of information that may provide evidence which could inform such decisions is only likely to be as good as the questions asked. The collection of information will be different in content and character if the child is bilingual. In fact, many EPs would claim that decisions cannot be made until such crucial basic information is collected (Robson 1991). However, there is often a wealth of information available, held by different people or stored in different files around the school, which, if put together, would build a useful picture of the child. Once questions have been asked and evidence collected together then more accurate decisions as to the nature of the appropriate support can be provided by the school.

Anna Wright (1991) puts the dilemma facing professionals in assessing a bilingual child with reported learning difficulties very clearly. She claims that this process involves avoiding two errors.

- False positive:
  the error of diagnosing a learning difficulty where none is present, therefore labelling the child and possibly changing the mode of instruction or environment to one that is not suitable, for example, by placing a child in a special school where the language environment may be less rich.
- False negative:
  the error of failing to diagnose a learning difficulty and thus not giving the child appropriate help at an early stage, allowing subsequent difficulties to become more entrenched and harder to manage.

11

Historical perspective

This neatly reflects the historical pattern of referral of bilingual children to special schools and units in this country. As early as the 1970s, representatives of Britain's minority communities expressed concern as to the over-representation of black and bilingual children in segregated provision. Coard (1971), Tomlinson (19812) and the Commission for Racial Equality (CRE) (1986) have all drawn attention to the fact that pupils whose home language was not 'standard English' were discriminated against in their allocation to separate or special educational provision (*false positive*).

In the 1980s, due to challenges to the racist assumptions which designated many bilingual children as having SEN in terms of their learning, there was an under-referral of these pupils to specialist provision. At the same time there was an increasing awareness of the linguistic and cultural bias of many of the standardised tests, both here and in the USA. Unfortunately, some bilingual children with extensive learning needs, and sometimes with considerable sensory loss, were therefore left for years before proper referral and assessment on the assumption that as they were bilingual they just needed 'more time' (*false negative*).

Hopefully, with a better understanding of the need for language support for targeted pupils within the mainstream classroom, and of the need to continually assess levels of additional language acquisition and learning across the curriculum, this situation is now being rectified.

As stated in Chapter 1, there is no reason to suppose that any more or less percentage of any one population is likely to experience SEN as defined by the 1981 Education Act (DES 1981) than any other. In fact, Circular 1/83 was at some pains to separate linguistic problems from learning difficulties and to specifically exclude those children whose sole difficulty was because the language of instruction was different from their home language. There is no doubt that proper identification and assessment of bilingual pupils has suffered from institutional and unjust practices in the past, and that disproportionate numbers of black and bilingual children were either wrongly assessed or left with unidentified difficulties.

Problems of standard psychological tests

There has been a realisation among many EPs of the inappropriateness of most standardised tests which would otherwise be employed as part of the assessment of intellectual or learning difficulties of pupils experiencing difficulty at school. There is no test that serves to answer the question of whether or not a bilingual child has learning difficulties, and EPs are very much reliant on the evidence presented by schools for the following reasons of inadequacy of the available tests.

Cultural bias

Standardised tests embody the Anglo-centric conformity by the assumption that everybody is a member of a homogeneous cultural and statistical population. It has already been argued that we live in a pluralistic society – we are aware that many of the ethnic and language minorities have been exposed to very different learning experiences from middle-class English children. This could equally apply to long-settled families as well as to recent arrivals.

Since all learning occurs within a culture, tests can be considered to be culture loaded because test construction procedures are inevitably based on the culture of the dominant group. Even if items were specifically picked to reflect the unique learning experiences of individual minority groups they would be rejected in the item analysis because they would be 'difficult' for the majority group and thus would not correlate well with the total test; i.e. in psychometric terminology they are not 'good' items. It is not difficult to see how this construction biases tests against minority groups. Even tests for young pre-school age children can make assumptions about the familiarity of play objects and experiences without the necessary awareness of cultural differences. The extent of any bias will depend on how different the socialisation/learning experiences of the child are from those of the majority in the representative sample.

Language bias

Verbal tests are particularly prone to bias, moreover it is virtually impossible to design a verbal test appropriate for all bilingual children that is free of bias. No generally accepted alternatives to the use of English IQ tests exist, which is why their use and interpretation is subject to such great caution by psychologists today. The use of Raven's Matrices (Raven *et al.*1998) (non-verbal ability) or the National Foundation for Educational Research (NFER) Cognitive Abilities Tests (Lohman *et al.* 2001) can sometimes throw up inter-test discrepancies between verbal and non-verbal behaviours. These can offer useful starting points for further investigations (Cline and Frederickson 1999). For example, a high non-verbal score and a low verbal score could indicate an early stage of language acquisition or a specific learning difficulty. On the other hand, weak non-verbal and verbal scores might simply indicate a bilingual pupil whose verbal talents have not been accurately reflected because of the language bias, rather than an indication of a general learning difficulty.

Even something so apparently simple as word association is fraught with difficulty as it depends on familiarity with the context and content of the problem.

Translation

Why, then, can tests not simply be translated from the English and administered by a native speaker? Apart from the arguments about cultural and linguistic bias, there are issues of differing syntax, which would render tests unreliable and invalid across varying translations, languages and dialects. Furthermore, as Cline (1998) points out, some children do not have academic language in their preferred language because this is not the vocabulary used at home.

Populations of norm-referenced tests

Some attempts have been made in parts of Britain to design and validate tests designed for one population of minority children in a geographical area, e.g.

Sandwell Bilingual Screening Assessment (Punjabi). This work on testing in minority languages has been pioneered by Speech and Language Services. However, this is mainly to help in the difficult field of ascertaining specific language disorders in bilingual children rather than in the more general area of the testing of academic potential. Such tests are standardised and validated on local minority language populations so they are inevitably rendered unreliable for children from other language communities.

There has been a recent revival in tests that are being designed partly in response to interest by LEAs in the concept of 'added value'. Due to the pressure from central government through standardised tests and published results, there is a need for greater accountability in order to prove the efficacy of teaching. As children start their formal schooling at such different stages of learning and experience, the use of baseline information is helpful as a starting point. It serves, at least, to say something about what part of their experiences pupils have learned from and to identify children's needs. This can give the teacher something to build upon at an early stage. It also serves to show how much progress is being made from a fixed point as a result of teaching.

Good baseline assessment should also give children opportunities to demonstrate knowledge, skills and understanding in ways that take account of their home language and cultures.

Introducing the 'map' (see photocopiable sheet on p. 77)

What is it?

The 'map' is a model or figure which begs the question as to whether a bilingual child is learning successfully at school. If there is any doubt about educational progress or confusion as to whether the child may have SEN, the map offers a route through which the various factors that may be causing a difficulty for a child learning in a second language can be explored. The following three chapters examine some of the existing theories and active ways in which teachers and schools can work towards a better informed decision by:

- asking questions
- collecting evidence
- planning support.

This map puts together and builds on the work and thinking from many different sources in the belief that greater awareness of issues makes for sound judgement.

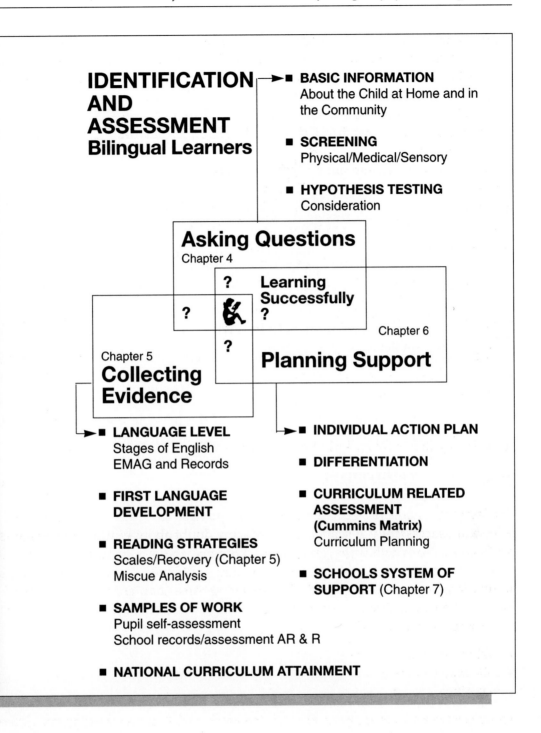

Why should we do it?

Ann Robson, a writer, researcher and senior EP, clearly states that she is unable to reach a decision about the learning of a bilingual child until crucial information has been checked. This is her list:

- family/child history
- perceptions of parents/family, child and teachers about learning progress and achievement

- physical health, medical information
- previous educational history and current education in school and community
- language knowledge and experience
- the context for learning in school and class
- evidence of a differentiated curriculum
- evidence of achievements to date, including samples of work
- evidence of other professionals involved
- community context and family status.

Without a full examination of the many possible factors that may be causing difficulty, we risk not addressing the bilingual child's real needs at an early enough point. Conversely, we also risk making wrong assumptions about a child's difficulty without first examining the adequacy of our own classroom practice. If good classroom practice is employed to include bilingual pupils in tasks set at an appropriate level of demand, with good visual access and opportunities to practise English language patterns in differing contexts, then pupils are likely to make good progress. It is out of concern for those pupils who don't have these opportunities that this map has been devised.

How to do it

Read the next three chapters that give some of the possible methodology which is often an inclusive part of normal good educational practice. You will raise your own level of awareness and in discussion with colleagues can use and adapt any of the material for your own purpose within school.

4 Asking questions: assessing background information

In this chapter the premise is made that the answer to concerns about a child's lack of learning progress will only be as good as the questions asked. Subsequent chapters will look at other parts of the model in terms of collecting evidence and providing support.

Basic communication about the child at home and in the community

What is it?

- Basic information that will help every school to assess the learning needs of a bilingual child on admission.

The school needs to collect such basic information when a pupil is first admitted. In most schools and LEAs, specific standardised admission information is required as a matter of course. For bilingual children, schools need fuller information than the biographical details required for monolingual pupils as this will have implications for teaching and learning.

Additional details should be sought on:

Languages

- What languages are used by individual members of the immediate family to the child?
- What languages are used by the child to them in return?
- Which languages can the child read? (Is the child learning to read?)
- Which languages can the child write? (Is the child learning to write?)

Social factors

- Information (and dates) about the number of terms of previous schooling in the UK.
- Information on previous schooling (and extent) abroad.
- Information on extended visits abroad, family separations (and dates).
- Details of names of both parents, names and ages of siblings.

- Details of family religion; festivals observed, dietary requirements.
- Family view of important illnesses or other medical factors seen as important.
- Community links
- Does the child attend any school/class/group in the community? How often?
- What is the name/address of the organisation?
- Who is the contact person for the group?
- What language is used/taught there?

Why should we do it?

- To provide a meeting point between parents and school.
- To provide a framework for discussion with parents.
- To emphasise the importance of working together to support the child's learning at school.
- To encourage the parents to continue to support first language development through story telling, sharing books and reading in the home language.
- To collect a full picture about the languages in which the child is living and learning outside school.

Good communication with parents should be established by the school as early as possible and the parents made to feel welcome.
Teachers need to be aware that:

- Parents' experiences of their own schooling may not always be positive ones!
- In some cultures parents are not expected or encouraged to participate in the process of their child's education at school.
- Some parents may have had little formal schooling in their own countries or may be illiterate in the standard form of their language.

How do we organise it?

Parents can be contacted by a home/school liaison teacher or by another adult worker at the school who speaks the home language. If absolutely necessary, most schools have access to translators who will be working within the community.

- Fill in an information form (see p. 19 and photocopiable sheet on p. 79). The headings will act as an aide-mémoire in seeking full details.
- Older pupils could simultaneously (or subsequently) be asked to fill in their own languages record (see p. 20 and photocopiable sheet on p. 80).
- Arrange a meeting. A relaxed informal atmosphere is essential and the meeting should be regarded as a gathering of information and discussion rather than conducted as a formal questionnaire.
- Parents should be encouraged to add any information that they feel is relevant.
- They may wish to bring a friend or extended family member to provide support and/or to act as an interpreter.
- The school should be clear where the information will be stored and who will have access to it.
- Emphasise that the focus of the meeting is to help their child make the most of the learning opportunities at school.

The Bilingual Pupil at Home and in the Community

Basic Family Details

Full Name .... D.O.B ....

Name child is called at home .... Age Now ....

Name to be called at school (if different) ....

Arrival date in UK (if not British born) ....

Length of previous school abroad ....

Names of schools/LEAs in UK ....

Number of terms of UK schooling...

Date of long extended absences from schooling ....

Place of birth .... Religion ....

Does child live with both parents as part of family unit? .... Festivals observed ....

If not who are carers?..

Mothers name .... Dietary needs ....

Fathers name ....

(School correspondence should be addressed to ....

Most useful written language for family is..

Names and ages of siblings ....

....

....

Languages

Languages spoken at home by pupil to   Mother............................ Grandparents.........................

       Father .... Siblings ....

Languages used by family members to child

Can child read/write languages other than English?   write .... read ....

Is child learning to read/write in languages other than English ....

Community Links

Does child attend any school/class in community/ ....

Mother tongue class .... community school .... religious .... Mosque/classes ....

What languages are used taught there? ....

What is the name/addresses of organisation? ....

....

....

Who is contact person for group?..

Is interpreter needed for teacher to communicate with parents? ....

If so, who might this be? ....

Family view of important illnesses/or other medical factors seen as important ....

Is child right handed? left handed? ....

Should child be using glasses hearing aid/other aids for learning? ....

Does child require any regular medication during school day ....

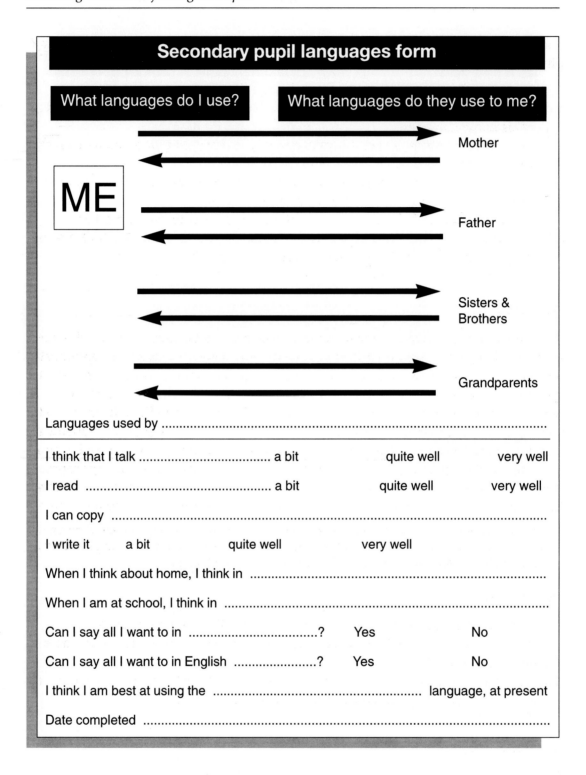

Secondary pupil languages form

| What languages do I use? | What languages do they use to me? |

ME

Mother

Father

Sisters & Brothers

Grandparents

Languages used by ....

I think that I talk .... a bit   quite well   very well

I read .... a bit   quite well   very well

I can copy ....

I write it   a bit   quite well   very well

When I think about home, I think in ....

When I am at school, I think in ....

Can I say all I want to in ....?   Yes   No

Can I say all I want to in English ....?   Yes   No

I think I am best at using the .... language, at present

Date completed ....

Screening for physical/sensory problems

What are they?

It is easy to assume that all children entering school have had full health and development checks prior to admittance – in the UK this is normally the case. However, where a bilingual pupil's learning is causing concern, one of the first questions to consider is whether the child's vision, hearing, general health and physical development are normal as they may not have had the usual screening.

- Does the child respond to her/his name being called?
- Does the child listen to and respond normally to other children and adults speaking her/his home language?
- Does the response from the child vary from day to day (good days and bad days)?
- Does the child seem particularly inattentive?
- Have you varied seating arrangements with a view to checking visibility of books, boards, easels used for class/group work and hearing?
- Does the child strain to see/have unusual difficulty copying from a model?
- Have you observed any unusual physical difficulties in physical education (PE) lessons?
- Have you checked and shared your concern with others?
- Have you checked with parents?

Why check this?

Children who were born in, or who have arrived from, other countries, or who have been transient, may have difficulties that have been missed or overlooked previously, yet which are serious enough to cause learning problems. It is not always easy to distinguish these if the child is new to English and if there are emotional or adjustment difficulties. Teachers' experience of children will usually indicate when to feel concern. Although teachers will need to arrange checks through the school nurse and child health agencies, they are often in the position of being able to provide clear evidence of the concern. It is vital that this concern is indicated to the appropriate professionals sooner rather than later. Trust your experience and the evidence! Bilingual children must not be left on the assumption that they 'just need more time'.

> NB Some conditions such as 'glue ear' are very common (one in every four children under five years). This causes intermittent hearing loss which can lead to serious problems in learning, particularly for a young child learning in a second language.

How to check

- Check with colleagues and others who speak the child's home language.
- Discuss your concern with parents. Have they noticed (by comparison to another child in the family)?
- Refer the child through the usual school channels to the school nurse. Ask them to check sight and hearing if there are no early health records.

Hypothesis testing

What is it?

This is a hypothesis testing approach developed by EPs as a response to some of the difficulties faced in the assessment of bilingual children who may have learning difficulties. The five-stage model below was developed by John Hutchins and the Educational Psychology Service in Tower Hamlets. It is included here to demonstrate how a hypothesis testing approach is helpful. It relies on the school collecting information and

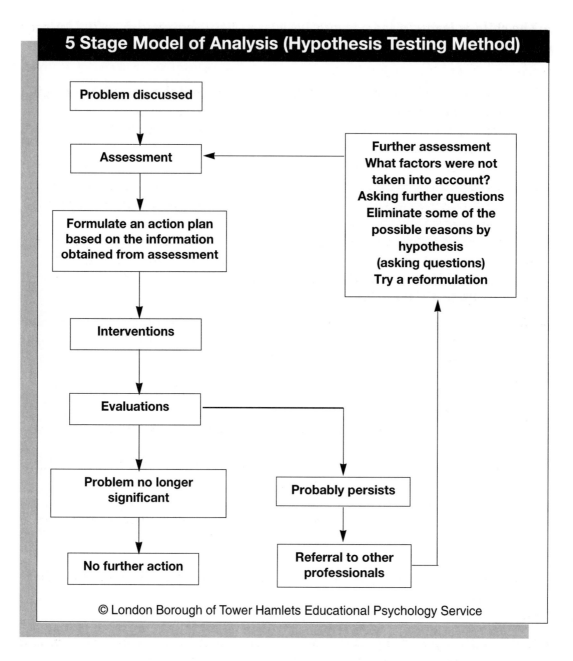

5 Stage Model of Analysis (Hypothesis Testing Method)

Problem discussed

↓

Assessment ←— Further assessment
What factors were not taken into account?
Asking further questions
Eliminate some of the possible reasons by hypothesis
(asking questions)
Try a reformulation

↓

Formulate an action plan based on the information obtained from assessment

↓

Interventions

↓

Evaluations

↓

Problem no longer significant   Probably persists

↓   ↓

No further action   Referral to other professionals

© London Borough of Tower Hamlets Educational Psychology Service

is a method of deciding what further information may be necessary to eliminate some of the possible reasons for, or causes of concern about, a child's lack of progress. This has been further developed (Wright 1991) as a list of possible reasons why a bilingual child may be failing at school. Each hypothesis comes with a list of suggested points to look at and consider. This does not represent a rigid, exhaustive framework; it is a tool to stimulate discussion and action. In order to test one hypothesis, others need to be disregarded in the first instance. This does not mean they must be disregarded permanently – they may need to be revisited. It should also be noted that more than one hypothesis may be true. Ignoring these possibilities could lead to a 'false negative' conclusion. For example, looking at hypothesis B: it would be a mistake to assume that, because a child has been traumatised, we can disregard the possibility that they have, for example, dyslexia.

A The child is learning more slowly because of basic factors to do with language development and/or task demands.

First considerations:

- The child may be learning more slowly because of limited experience in English. (Remember the timescale involved in second language development. Note the implications from the research on bilingual pupils listed in Chapter 2.)
- How long has the child been in school/exposed to English?
- The child may not be learning because basic proficiency in any language is not established and neither language has been given an adequate opportunity to develop. (Remember that first language skills are a valuable means of supporting a child's learning.)
- The child may not be learning because the level of basic conversational English has misled the teacher into setting tasks that are too abstract for the child's current language level. (See the model based on the work of Cummins (1984) in Chapter 6.)
- Consider the age of the child.

Initially disregard if:

- The child has been at school in this country and learning English for more than five years.
- There is an unusual pattern or structure to the child's language development. (See Hypothesis C.)
- The child is supported by home language teaching and is reportedly making good progress.
- The child's first language seems as well developed as for other bilingual children from the community of the same age.
- Context-embedded, concrete learning experiences are frequently provided within the classroom and the child can understand and express themselves well in relation to them.

B The child is not learning because of environmental stress experience inside or outside school.

First considerations:

- Is the child experiencing the ethos and curriculum of the school as alien and challenging rather than welcoming, accommodating and inclusive?
- Is the child or family experiencing overt or covert racism at home or at school?
- There may be trauma, for example, refugee children who have recent experience of horrific events such as civil war, or family separation and bereavement.
- Is the child being rejected by others or being subjected to conflicting demands from parents and peers?
- Is the family under particular stress due to housing or financial difficulties?

Initially disregard if:

- The school has a strong multicultural approach to teaching and there is evidence within it of the value placed on the languages and cultural backgrounds of all its pupils.

- There are good staff–parent, staff–pupil, pupil–pupil and school–community relationships together with a lot of contact with adult home language speakers.
- The child seems to have good self-esteem, is happy, supported and well motivated.
- There is no evidence of specific racist incidents. (Check with parents if you suspect this may be the case.)

C The child is failing because of a specific language disorder.
First considerations:

- The sequence in which the child is acquiring language compared with the stages of second language learning and the order in which children normally acquire this.
- The ways in which both languages are used to and by the child in various oral situations.
- The evidence of a bilingual speaker on the child's expressive and receptive skills in first language.
- The pragmatic language skills of the child.

Initially disregard if:

- The child is experiencing a loss of contact with their first/home language.
- The child has only been exposed to English for a short time (up to six months).
- No advantage is found in using non-verbal methods in systematic attempts to teach the child concepts.

  NB: *Only a very small percentage of children are statistically likely to have a specific language disorder (less than 1 per cent)*

D The child has Special Educational Needs as defined by the 1981 and 1993 Education Acts.
First considerations:

- The information on the child's learning over time.
- The child's learning and language profile and information on the strategies used by the child across the curriculum.
- How much of the curriculum is context embedded?

Initially disregard if:

- There are a number of other factors that might explain the child's failure to learn apart from lack of ability or specific learning difficulty.

Why do it?

- There is a better chance of accurate and well-informed assessment when more questions are posed and when greater evidence is collected.
- This method could give a structure to an early warning or concern meeting at which teachers share their concern about an individual child's lack of learning progress.
- The focus is on looking at the learning environment as much as at the child.
- Simpler reasons are unlikely to be overlooked.
- The child is less likely to be inaccurately labelled.

How to do it

- Work through the listed possible hypotheses for the child's perceived learning difficulties.
- Note down information gathered during the exercise together with areas where answers are unknown or where further information is required.
- Also note down any information and evidence that would appear to rule out the hypothesis in the first instance. You may wish to reconsider it later.
- Work with colleagues as a brainstorming session. You will stimulate each other's thinking!
- Add any other hypotheses or issues pertinent to your school or the child's situation that you feel have not been included or previously checked.

5 Collecting the evidence

In this chapter it is proposed that both primary and secondary schools already collect a wealth of information about pupils' learning in many ways. Listed below are just some of the ways in which evidence may be collected on bilingual pupils in schools. It is not inclusive – there are many other systems in use.

Assessing language stages

What are they?

Language stages are largely derived from the work of Hilary Hester and Inner London colleagues at the Centre for Language in Primary Education (CLPE) and first appeared in the *Primary Language Record Handbook* (Barrs *et al.* 1988). Many schools use a model based on Hester's four stages of English to identify pupils' current levels of English (baseline assessment) and as a means of charting progress across time.

These four stages are described as follows:

- Stage 1   new to English
- Stage 2   becoming familiar with English
- Stage 3   becoming confident as a user of English
- Stage 4   a very fluent user of English in most social and learning contexts

and are followed by a descriptive paragraph of active statements of observable behaviour typical of a (primary) bilingual pupil at each stage.

English as a second language (ESL) teachers may be more familiar with earlier descriptors such as beginner, elementary, intermediate and advanced, as second language textbooks, usually aimed at adult learners, are organised into four stages in this way. These generally correlate with the stages given above.

Why use them?

The purpose of regularly reviewing pupils' language levels is to monitor expected progress across time in the acquisition of English. Continuous teacher assessment is the best method of doing this. It is important that this is seen as part of the school's assessment recording and reporting procedure in showing pupils' attainment in

National Curriculum terms. Reports written in isolation from the body of the mainstream teaching and learning would be limited in value. Where class/subject teachers contribute to these records, they can be used as a diagnostic tool to analyse needs for a future teaching focus. Language stages are also used in many LEAs to provide baseline information for statistical purposes.

Language stages are also used for statistical purposes to support funding under the Ethnic Minority Achievement Grant. The language stage statistics are used to demonstrate the numbers of bilingual pupils at each stage, both in order to show progress and to demonstrate the need for continued funding for their support. This can be viewed as somewhat of a contradiction in terms! However, the results of these analyses are useful to target additional language support more precisely to student needs within an individual institution and also provide discussion/moderation between schools.

How to assess language acquisition

Use the Hester stages as a guide for discussion with colleagues, together with your knowledge of National Curriculum expectations and experience of bilingual pupils' normal acquisition of English.

- Design a method of recording progress that fits/is complementary with the current system within the school. (No one will welcome additional/separate systems!) Continuous teacher assessment and some structured and systematic targeting will focus teaching on aspects that need attention within the curricular framework.
- Create a forum for debate about the nature and expectation of language across the curriculum, subject-specific language and appropriate methodologies that will involve bilingual pupils in language activities.

Teachers and departments supporting bilingual learners at secondary schools often have considerable experience and knowledge of patterns of typical errors made by bilingual pupils from one language community. These relate to the structural differences of the first language.

Typical errors in English made by Bengali or Sylheti speakers

An example of an information sheet for Bengali is included as a model (see pp. 29 and 30). Similar information could be collected, checked with the minority language speakers for accuracy, and distributed to staff in your school/authority. The errors made by most bilingual pupils are likely to fit this pattern and will give a 'norm'. If a pupil's errors deviate widely from this then further investigation should be made as it may be indicative of a specific disorder.

These North Indian/Bangladeshi languages are derived from Sanskrit and belong to the Indo Ayrian language group.

Children learning to speak English as their second language will often display errors that occur as a result of applying grammatical (syntactical) rules of their home/first language to English.

These structural errors are transient and on their own do **not** mean that the child has a language disorder. However, if the errors continue beyond a couple of years and there is other evidence of difficulty in receptive and expressive language, a child may need to be assessed by the Speech and Language Service. (These difficulties would also be evident in L1 so a bilingual assessment is desirable.)

As children become more competent in English they will also make errors that are typical, common, developmental errors of monolingual children – particularly in the use of grammatical rules.

Grammatical differences

- The basic word order in a sentence is **subject – object – verb** (SOV) compared to the English order of SVO.
- There is no definite (the) article or indefinite (a) article before the noun.
- Post-positions are used instead of prepositions.
- The third person pronoun is the same for masculine and feminine gender. Verb inflection usually signals gender.
- A second form of the second person pronoun is used with elders/strangers as a mark of respect.
- Bengali uses gender for neutral/natural nouns e.g. sun (masculine); moon, river (feminine).
- The verb component of a sentence can consist of one, two or three parts. The first part of the verb is in root form which is inflectioned to signify tense.
- Adverbs usually precede the noun.

Typical errors

- Putting verbs at the end of sentences.
  'He crayons not giving'

- Leaving out articles before a noun
  'She give me sweet'

- Using prepositions after a noun or inserting them where unnecessary.
  'I told to my mum'

- Confusing placement of plurals, especially noun-adjective concord.
  'bigs girls'

- Incorrect use of third person pronouns, particularly over-use of
  'he', 'him'

- Inappropriate use of 'no', 'not'.
  'He no play with me', 'I not got my pencil'

- Omitting auxiliary verb.
  'My dad going Bangladesh', 'He reading'

- Placing adverbs or adverbial phrases inappropriately.
  'He too much cursing'

- Wrong use (or lack) of preposition.

'He hit me in my arm'

NB

- Bengali writing **hangs** on the line while English writing **sits** on the line.
- Bengali script does not distinguish between capital and lower case letters.

As we have seen, the whole subject of assessment is fraught with difficulty, however there have been many local developments in methods of assessing bilingual pupils' stages of English.

Most of the local stage models have separated each stage into the four language skills of National Curriculum English: reading, writing, speaking and listening (the latter two are often amalgamated). In the case of Tower Hamlets, the secondary framework for assessment eventually agreed upon locally was of particular benefit to those newly in post or where schools had not yet developed strong systems. It was particularly pleasing that the framework was flexible enough to be used in various ways by departments in different schools after a period of piloting with new Year 7 intakes. Three examples follow:

- School 1 used the statement bank to create an A4 fourfold recording sheet for every targeted bilingual pupil where statements were highlighted in a different colour each term to show progress at a glance (see pp. 32, 33 and 34).
- School 2 used the proforma as an in-service education and training (INSET) tool with a subject department that provided some discussion, training and considerable awareness-raising about language activities and achievement within the subject area.
- School 3 put the statement bank onto their department/school computer network which is updated termly.

Recent developments

The QCA has developed EAL step descriptors that assess bilingual pupils' National Curriculum English. There are four steps: Step 1, Step 2, Level One (Threshold) and Level One (Secure). Following these four steps, pupils move on to Level Two of the National Curriculum for English. Each step is a broad description of English language behaviour in speaking, listening, reading and writing.

The step descriptors differ from assessment carried out by EAL teachers in some respects. EAL teachers usually aim for a detailed description of how each pupil uses English socially and academically to access the whole curriculum and to function as a member of the school community whereas the step descriptors are confined to National Curriculum English. EAL teachers feel that step descriptors alone give insufficient information about a pupil's language behaviour and support needs – especially important if pupils have learning difficulties.

Some work has been done in a number of authorities to develop a system in which step descriptors can be used in conjunction with stages of language acquisition (see above). The QCA step descriptors can be extended to take account of these stages of EAL acquisition. Early work has helped to highlight discrepancies between pupil attainment on the English National Curriculum (used on its own) and the extended form of the step descriptors (taking EAL stages into account). Pupils may legitimately achieve higher scores on National Curriculum English levels than on extended step descriptors. This reveals that needs for intervention and support are not reflected in the English National Curriculum when it is used alone. This mismatch highlights the need for certain kinds of classroom support for bilingual pupils at the higher levels, e.g. scaffolding and collaborative activities. In simple terms, accurate assessment of pupils' language skills and support needs requires information about their language behaviour across all curriculum areas, not simply English.

The most up-to-date information on this developing situation can be gathered from local Ethnic Minority Achievement (EMA) teams or from the professional organisations that represent them. Examples of these include Northern Association of Support Services for Equality and Achievement and NALDIC (see Useful addresses).

Assessing first language development

What is it?

It may be useful here to clarify some terms. 'First language' (L1) replaced 'mother tongue' as a label for the language the pupil feels most confident in using. This is often the home language that the pupil learned first. In order to acknowledge the variety of experiences and life histories of our pupils, many educators use the term 'preferred language'.

Most schools give pupils who speak a home language other than English, and who are new to the school or new to English, some form of internally designed initial assessment test. This is widely agreed to be helpful in establishing the learner's competence in English and provides a basis for immediate and future additional teaching. It can identify areas for development and establish short or longer term targets by identifying what a child knows, understands and can do in addition to their current competence in English. Such tests are vital when a child is admitted to school as a 'casual entry' but less necessary when a child transfers with records and samples of work from another local school. Some of the dangers of assessing English can be minimised if the assessment can be carried out with the help of a trained first-language speaker.

Some young children who have been born in the UK have been exposed to little or no English before school. A first language assessment can be particularly useful in diagnosing language difficulty for those pupils whose learning progress is already causing concern compared with other bilingual peers from a similar background. Assessing children in their first language can also help to sort out whether the lack of adequate progress is concerned with the acquisition of an additional language or whether conceptual or information processing difficulties are present. It can work as an indicator to guide monolingual teachers in arranging more appropriate support for diagnosed difficulties.

Assessment of bilingual learners

Language Assessment Log ESL Department

SCHOOL: _____

Name and Surname: _____

Tutor Group: _____

Date of Entry into School: _____

Years of Schooling in Britain: _____

First Language: _____

Date of Assessment/Colour Code:

200 _____ Autumn Term _____ Orange _____

Spring Term _____ Green _____

Summer Term _____ Yellow _____

Curriculum area subject/through which language development is assessed:

_____

Assessment completed by _____ (Teacher's name)

Assessment of (secondary) bilingual learners

STAGE ONE

Listening	Speaking	Reading	Writing

a) Listens and responds to
 	
    questions
    commands
    instructions
 	
in L1
non-verbally
	a) is silent in class
	
	b) speaks predominantly in first language
	
	c) intitiates
	
	    single words
	    short phrases
	    asks simple
	    questions
		a) recognises letters
		
		b) sounds out words
		
		c) reads simple words
		
		d) recognises words in context
		
		e) relies on pictures for meaning
		
		f) reads for meaning
			a) forms letters
			
			b) attempts task via copying
			
			c) remembers spelling of some basic words
			
			d) spells phonetically
			
			e) relies on structure of given model
			
			f) begins to write independently.

STAGE TWO

Listening	Speaking	Reading	Writing
a) still requires reiteration of instructions b) can retrieve specific information from teacher/group talk c) follows simple instructions and explanations	a) converses in informal situations b) begins to participate in group work	a) retrieves specific information from passage b) attempts unknown words c) begins to guess meaning of unknown words from context d) able to read and discuss text	a) begins to punctuate b) can write short passages using prompts as guide c) shows some under-standing of spelling patterns d) can sequence work in a logical order e) shows awareness of rule system e.g. tenses

STAGE THREE

Listening	Speaking	Reading	Writing

a) clearly understands great amount of teacher and peer talk
 	
b) follows complex explanations
 	
c) needs less support in comprehension and execution of tasks required
	a) shows confidence in initiation and sustaining a conversation
	
	b) shows confidence about reporting back in different situations
	
	c) beginning to vary language according to audience
	
	d) performs broad range of language functions such as questioning and predicting
	
	e) use of spoken language is still in advance of literacy
		a) reads more complex texts with much understanding
		
		b) manages with mainstream materials but may still require some support
		
		c) reads aloud with speed, confidence and fluency but not always with appropriate expression
			a) can write independently although writing may still show errors in:
			    specific vocabulary
			    spelling and punctuation
			    grammatical relationships
			
			b) attempts to express complex ideas but clarity often blurred by above areas
			
			c) beginning to develop appropriate styles and registers
			
			d) is aware of linguistic limitations and occasionally frustrated by them

STAGE FOUR

Listening	Speaking	Reading	Writing
a) fluent bilingual		a) able to read a range of materials confidently b) able to skim and scan	a) can confidently under-take a range of different types of writing b) shows influence of extended reading when writing

Assessment of bilingual learners

LANGUAGE STAGE

		Speaking	Listening	Reading	Writing
LEVEL	**Beginner**				
	1				
	2				
	3				
	4				

Why do it?

Many schools/LEAs employ bilingual assistants who can be trained and supported to administer a school-developed test in a child's first language. Where a young child's learning is causing concern, this would help to establish whether the child's first language is delayed or poorly developed. If this is the case, remediation can be given by the bilingual assistant using both languages and progress closely monitored by the teacher. This is a valuable and focused use of their skills in the classroom.

- Poorly developed L1 may be an important indicator of SEN. In any case, a child whose first language is not well developed by school age will be severely disadvantaged in learning an additional language and targeted support could prevent learning failure at a critical early stage.

How to assess first language

- Methods that can assess the child's first language communication skills in terms of the expectations of normal classroom language activities – such as retelling stories, sequencing pictures, listening and acting upon simple instructions – will also provide information on the use of linguistic structures such as tense. If similar material has been trialled with bilingual children of the same age and background within the school who are making good progress in their learning then some local norms will quickly be established.
- The use of an audio-tape recording of the children's performance can be invaluable for discussion, trialling agreement and training purposes with colleagues.
- Using a bilingual member of staff who is familiar to the children and who has worked in the classroom will be less threatening to the child being assessed. It is also important to note when and to what extent the child was prompted, together with affective factors such as whether the child seemed anxious, unwell, confident and so on.

A model of a first oral language assessment form is included here as an example of one primary school's work in this field (see p. 36). It was developed and trialled over the course of two terms by a working party consisting of the deputy head (also the special educational needs coordinator (SENCO)); the school Section 11 coordinator (*note* funding previously received through Section 11 is now delivered through the Ethnic Minority Achievement Grant); the bilingual instructor; the reading recovery trained teacher and Deryn Hall. It also involved discussion with the school's EP, the principal EP, a bilingual assessment teacher and the local Speech and Language Service. It is offered here, not as a definitive assessment test but as an example of the sort of assessment that can be developed to suit local needs. The materials used for the test were two Brian Wildsmith picture story books without words, *The Nest* and *The Apple Bird* (copies of which were in the classroom and familiar to the pupils), and some everyday objects common to both cultures.

The school used the test to assess and work intensively with Year 1 and 2 children causing concern in three ways.

- Some children were found to have poorly developed first language skills and the bilingual instructor worked with the children and their families to provide additional first language support.

First Language Assessment

SCHOOL: _____

Children causing concern: First Language Assessment Year 1/2
Remember to praise child after each task!

Name: _____ **Year:** _____ **Date of Birth:** _____

Date: _____ **Assessed by:** _____

Task 1   Narrative (The Nest)

	Good	OK	Poor	Prompt

Look at these pictures. They tell a story.
Can you tell me what is happening?
PROMPT. . . .   What is happening here? Tell me.

Comments:

Task 2   Sequencing (The Applebird)

These pictures make a story too.
They are all muddled up.
Can you put them in order to tell a story?
PROMPT. . .   Which picture do you think comes first?
*   Which picture comes next?*

Left to right

Comments:

Task 3   Relating personal experience

	Good	OK	Poor	Prompt

Tell me what you did . . .   in class this morning.
(at home last night,
before you come to school this morning,
in the playground at break)

Comments:

Task 4   Comprehension

Now we are going to do something different. I am going to ask you to give me something from the things on the table. Listen carefully to what I ask you to do. Are you ready . . . . (Child's name). . .?

Give me the thing I need .... to open the door   key
What did you give me?

Give me the thing I need .... to eat my food   spoon
What did you give me?

Give me the thing I need .... to write in my book   pen
What did you give me?

Give me the thing I need .... to cut paper   scissors
What did you give me?

Give me the thing I need .... to comb my hair   comb
What did you give me?

Task 5   Following verbal instructions

Now I am going to ask you to do something else. Look at the things in front of you. Listen carefully. OK. Ready?

Put the spoon in the jar.
Put the scissors on the floor.
Put the key under your chair.

Put the spoon on the table and the key in the jar.
Put the pen on the chair and the scissors on the table.

Put the spoon in the jar, take the key out of the jar and put the key on top of the scissors.

Take the spoon out of the jar and put the jar on the carpet. Put the pen in the jar.

Task 6   Memory

I'm going to say some numbers. I want you to repeat them after I've finished.
(Stop when the child has got two of them wrong.)

2 5	7 3
8 1 6	9 4 5
7 2 9 6	4 1 3 8
6 4 2 1 7	3 9 7 5 8

ADDITIONAL COMMENTS:

Was the child:	nervous cooperative	tired confident	shy unwell	anxious lacking concentration

- Other children were assessed as having satisfactory or first language skills. These were then targeted by the Section 11 teachers (see previous note on Section 11) for more structured help in acquiring English.
- Some children showed weaknesses in certain of the assessed areas. They were subsequently included in small group activities to remediate these.

Reading strategies

What are they?

As young children develop as readers and their knowledge, experience and understanding of texts increases, they move along a continuum from dependence to independence (Barrs *et al*. 1988). 'Becoming a reader: Reading Scale 1' suggests a simple way of recording a young child's progress along a dimension from being reliant on an adult reading a text aloud, to greater confidence in deciphering familiar and the unfamiliar texts for themselves. From the same source 'Reading Scale 2' gives information about a child's experience as a reader across the curriculum on a separate scale and is useful for older pupils from Year 3 onwards.

Psycholinguists describe the range of cue systems in the English language as follows:

- Semantic cues – using previous knowledge of stories and texts to predict words, events, phrases that are likely to make the text make sense; i.e. 'meaning' cues.
- Syntactic cues – relying on knowledge and experience of patterns in spoken and written language (grammar) to predict text; i.e. structural language cues.
- Graphophonic cues – applying knowledge and experience of the relationships between sounds and symbols to decipher particular words; i.e. print cues. *These are sometimes augmented by the term* visual cues, *referring to whole-word recognition.*

Experienced readers apply a combination of these strategies in order to read. Clay (1979) claims that 'all readers, from five year old beginners on their first books to the effective adult reader need to use: the meaning; the sentence structure; order cues; size cues; special features; special knowledge; first and last letter cues before they resort to left to right sounding out chunks or letter clusters, or in the last resort, single letters'. Clay goes on to state that 'Such an analysis makes the terms "look and say" or "sight words" or "phonics" nonsense as complete explanations of all we need to know or do in order to be able to read'. Weaver (1980) shows how these strategies are combined in a process that follows a repeating cycle of prediction, sampling, confirming and correcting. Reading is clearly more than just a sum of its parts even when there is agreement as to what these parts are, and readers need to experience a wide range of texts to achieve critical literacy.

Why are they important?

Knowledge of the strategies employed by the child will usefully inform the teacher as to where appropriate support can be given to aid understanding and fluency when reading. This is important for bilingual pupils in learning English as they may be gaining literacy in more than one language. The dependence–independence and inexperienced–experience scales (Barrs *et al.* 1988) give useful information about knowledge of a language other than English, especially if noted by a bilingual teacher who shares the child's home language. Noting the reading strategies employed by the child would also help to prevent the phenomena frequently observed in the lower secondary school whereby pupils appear to decipher unseen print with fluency yet understand little of the text that they are 'reading'. Awareness of the individual reading style of the pupil means that support can be focused on the nature of the learning task.

How to analyse reading behaviour

'Miscue analysis' is a method of analysing what children do as they read an unseen text aloud. Based on the work of Goodman (1973) and subsequently adapted by others (including Barrs *et al.* 1988), it is a means of recording the errors and self-corrections made by the child as s/he processes the text. The successful strategies used when reading can then be identified together with the negative strategies that may be hindering a general understanding of the text. It uses the three-way cue system of psycholinguistics mentioned above. The only difference in approach for a bilingual child might be the focus on the degree of structure, detail, systematic teaching and continuous assessment/record keeping in activities that emphasise meaning. It is preferable to work from a familiar or discussed text as in 'reading recovery'.

'Reading recovery' is an individual teaching programme for the early detection of reading difficulties based on the work of Marie Clay (1979). It is usually offered to young pupils of approximately six years-old, selected for additional support by trained, supervised teachers. Part of the teacher's time is funded specifically for the systematic observation and teaching programme as part of a school's commitment to reducing reading difficulties. Twenty-six authorities in Britain have funding for official Reading Recovery schemes, however the term is sometimes used in a more generalised (and unofficial) way for less rigorous programmes. The reason for mentioning it here is that it provides very detailed and closely monitored information on the child's reading, writing and spelling strategies. If a bilingual pupil has been selected for this individual teaching (usually 30 minutes daily), the very full information yielded will be a valuable part of any assessment of literacy.

Samples of work: pupil profiles

What are they?

An experienced teacher can often tell a great deal more about a child's level of learning from an annotated piece of work than from detailed reports. Unfortunately teachers have not always been encouraged to trust their years of experience which, in fact, gives them many benchmarks against which to judge learning performance more reliably than a single test result. In the same way, samples of a pupil's work taken across time and across the curriculum can be more revealing than standardised test results.

The 'Records of Achievement' movement for secondary pupils aimed to record pupil's success in all aspects of their school life, not merely academic success. Pupils leaving school at the end of their statutory school life, sometimes with little in the way of exam results, were able to take with them a record that included samples of work.

In the same way as continuous teacher assessment records learning development across time, so portfolios, profiles and work samples can map the development of pupil's learning in English as a second language. At a local INSET session to 'moderate' language stages at secondary stage, teachers brought in samples of pupils' work from different curriculum areas that they felt were representative of Stages 1 to 4. This led to very useful discussion about standard errors and the skills demanded for extended writing in humanities at Key Stage 4, among other issues. Such meetings present good opportunities for teachers to discuss ways of scaffolding writing in their own curriculum areas.

Why do it?

A pupil profile or collection of samples of work is intended to demonstrate progress across time. This gives important information about:

- rate (speed) of progress
- types of errors being made
- familiarity with the variety of written forms demanded by different curriculum areas.

This information can be used diagnostically to inform teachers how to target support, and can help them to observe when a plateau of learning occurs (usually Stage 2 or 3) so that they can minimise educational underachievement in pupils who would be capable of better results at the end of Key Stage 4.

How to collect samples of work

Many secondary schools have collected samples of coursework to use in moderation exercises. OFSTED inspectors expect to see some pupils' work across the curriculum for the school year, and profiles of samples of core curriculum work are kept as a matter of course by many primary schools as part of their continuous assessment. The method for keeping the work is as varied as the institutions involved, but the main reason is for clarity and agreement about:

- what to keep
- how to annotate it (date, subject, first draft, corrected, unaided, with support?)
- how it is to be stored (so that it is accessible, where and in what container?)
- how often to sample
- why it is being done (relationship to assessment, recording and reporting?).

Pupil self-assessment

What is it?

This is related to the above section as pupils should be closely involved in the monitoring and selection of their work samples.

Why encourage this?

Involving pupils in some responsibility for their own learning is more likely to lead to better motivation for intrinsic rewards and greater independence. As pupils learn a greater self-reliance by negotiating and taking pride in their learning, their involvement in objective self-assessment can empower them as learners. Even young pupils are capable of evaluating their work, reflecting on their own progress and acknowledging strengths and weaknesses.

How to do it

- build this into your reporting and recording systems
- use self-assessment sheets at the end of lessons/units of work (see p. 42)
- through conferencing (a structured, recorded meeting of pupil and teacher).

   NB *The Revised Draft Code of Practice 2000 (DfEE 2000a) strongly recommends that pupils are consulted in target setting at all Code of Practice stages. It does recognise, however, that 'no presumptions should be made about levels of understanding and communication'. Schools therefore have a responsibility to organise support where necessary.*

School records/assessments

What are they?

These are the systems in place in schools which OFSTED inspectors will examine for evidence of the methods used for pupils' 'assessment, recording and reporting' (known as AR&R). There is often a mass of information about bilingual pupils' learning in different parts of the school's record systems which, if put together in one place, would provide comprehensive evidence of whether there was cause for concern of SEN.

Why do it?

Some of these are legal requirements:

- School records must be kept on every pupil's progress and these must be updated at least once a year.
- Schools must provide a written report to parents at least once a year, including National Curriculum assessments.
- Pupils' achievements in public examinations must be made available for publication.

Self-Assessment Sheet

Topic _____ Subject _____

Name _____ Class _____

The work I enjoyed doing most was _____

_____

because _____

I think I do best when _____

_____

because _____

The work I am most proud of is _____

_____

because_____

The work I found most difficult was _____

_____

because _____

I think I am quite good at these skills _____

_____

because_____

I think I need to work on these skills _____

_____

Signature _____ Date _____

- Schools are required to assess National Curriculum subjects at or near the end of each Key Stage.

Apart from these, school records measure the progress of bilingual pupils compared to their peers. The amount of time spent in learning English is a key factor in the consideration that needs to be given to the pupil's learning needs.

How to do it

The *Handbook for the Inspection of Schools* (OFSTED 1994a) sets expectations about this:

- whatever the individual arrangements made by the school, they need to be manageable
- the outcomes need to inform future work and be written in a way which is constructive and helpful to teachers, pupils and their parents
- the school's arrangements for AR&R will result in accurate and consistent records of achievement of individual pupils in relation to National Curriculum attainment targets.

National Curriculum assessments

What are they?

These consist of teacher assessments of the National Curriculum core subjects as to the levels of attainment (ATs) demonstrated by the pupils on the programmes of study (PoS) laid down. Pupils are also assessed by standard assessment tests (SATs). They are externally prescribed and set across the country at the same time to pupils of similar ages at the end of three of the four Key Stages. These are set at age 7 (Year 2); age 11 (Year 6) and age 14 (Year 9). Two more recent developments in National Curriculum assessment are: first, the increased formality of measurement of Early Learning Goals, and secondly the use of P scales to assess progress at or below the lowest National Curriculum performance indicators. The latter offers some measure of progress for some pupils with SEN where previous measures had failed.

Why do it?

You have no choice! Schools are required to assess pupils in National Curriculum core subjects under the Education Reform Act (1988). Guidance is set out in various DfEE circulars from subsequent years. As this is mandatory it is important that whatever systems are in place for the assessment of bilingual pupils they fit with this requirement in order to:

- involve curriculum members of staff
- minimise additional workloads
- ensure that bilingual pupils are assessed as part of mainstream curriculum.

How to do it

We know that assessment and testing of any child is complex and controversial. The central issue for bilingual pupils revolves around the question of how any assessment can be fair and accurate if conducted in a language that is not familiar to the child. The real challenge is how to overcome the gap between what the child knows and is capable of and her/his performance in a second language, which may act as a barrier to a demonstration of achievement. One solution would be to assess the child in the first language and the DfEE has conceded that 'special arrangements' may be made for standard national tests whereby:

- A trained, fluent first language support teacher can help with the assessments for science and maths. They may provide oral translation of certain words or phrases and simplify the written instructions in line with the 'Test Guidance Notes' distributed to schools.
- Pupils may, at the head teacher's discretion, use bilingual dictionaries or word lists as long as these do not provide any subject assistance, i.e. they cannot be used for English tests.

6 Planning support

All schools have a duty to support the learning of all their pupils, acknowledging individual differences and learning needs in their planning and provision. For bilingual pupils, much support is available through the methodologies and good practice considered earlier in this handbook. In this chapter, another method of supporting individual pupils is considered together with one inclusive planning tool that has a particular relevance for bilingual pupils whose learning is causing concern.

Individual action plans

What are they?

Individual action plans (IAPs) have long been used by special needs teachers to plan and monitor specific interventions with pupils who are giving cause for concern. These have now become a formal part of the school – based stages of 'School Action' and 'School Action Plus' in the Revised Draft Code of Practice (DfEE 2000a) – and renamed as individual education plans (IEPs).

The IEP should set out:

- the short-term targets for the pupil
- the teaching strategies to be used
- the provision to be put in place
- when the plan is to be reviewed
- the outcome of the action taken.

However, an IAP (this term should be used to distinguish it from any direct association with SEN) can be written for any pupil by any teacher whenever there is a need to focus some short-term additional support for learning for a pupil. It is simply a systematic action plan based on teachers' skills of observation and agreed with the pupil concerned.

Why use them?

The reality of most classrooms is for pupils to work in groups, however for the exceptional case where a pupil does not seem to be making the expected progress, an

IAP can help pinpoint the problem. The emphasis on a systematic approach automatically means that some focused thinking, planning and action is likely to occur. Most pupils would benefit from this although the majority of bilingual pupils will not require it. Bilingual pupils causing learning concern should make accelerated progress as a result of a specific action plan if it is properly executed. Those who don't may have some greater difficulty, which will need to be referred (see p. 47).

How to use them

IAPs can be used as a systematic approach for any pupil causing concern by any teacher following this plan. It is particularly useful if you work with a colleague to:

- clarify and define the problem using your skills of observation and reflection
- collect evidence about the concern (what the pupil can/cannot do)
- plan what to do, when and who will do it: set achievable targets
- act on it
- review progress, refocus targets.

Action plans need to be 'SMART' i.e.:

S   **Specific**
M   **Measurable**
A   **Attainable**
R   **Relevant**
T   **Time-constrained**

Supporting bilingual pupils through inclusive practice in the curriculum

What is it?

The supplements on inclusive practice in the National Curriculum Handbooks (DfEE 1999a, 1999b) set out:

> three principles that are essential to developing a more inclusive curriculum:
>
> A Setting suitable learning challenges
> B Responding to pupils' diverse learning needs
> C Overcoming potential barriers to learning and assessment for individuals and groups of pupils.
>
> (DfEE 1999a: 32)

It is important to remember that memberships of these groups are neither discrete nor permanent. They could be affected by the nature and demands of the learning activity and the individual pupil's needs, which could be long or short term. Research on learning styles (e.g. Gardner 1993) has become increasingly influential in the classroom and many teachers are finding that planning to accommodate this diversity enhances pupils' access to a wider variety of learning experiences. These approaches are also reflected in the work of practitioners such as Susan Hart (2000)

Individual Action Plan

For _____ Start date _____

Class _____ Review date _____

Area of work

Evidence

Plan

Action taken

Individual Action Plan (Teacher's Notes)

For _____ Start date _____

Class _____ Review date _____

Area of work

involve pupil if possible

- Clarify and define problem
- Pin it down to a specific area of curriculum, skill and activity
- Specify the difficulty as clearly as possible.

Evidence

involve pupil if possible

- Define present level of skill in area
- What can pupil do/not do?
- What strategies does pupil use?
- What are pupil's strengths?

Plan

involve pupil if possible

- Write down exactly what you intend pupil to do
- (make it small steps, observable and measurable)
- When will it happen? (daily? twice a week?)
- For how long? how often?
- Where?
- Who will help pupil? (teacher? helper? group? peer?)

Action taken

- Use this space to record any outcomes, problems, changes made
- Report back at review with evidence of pupil's learning during 'Action Plan' period

and Jim Cummins (1996), who emphasise the importance of 'reviewing what is generally provided for all [learners]', given the constantly changing map of classroom needs.

Why do it?

> All children deserve to have to have their achievements and progression recognised and the curriculum should reflect the different levels of attainment likely to be achieved.
> (DfEE 1999c: 48)

Access to the curriculum is an equal opportunities issue for pupils. This is their entitlement to reach their learning potential. Bilingual pupils are capable of high achievement if appropriate demands, materials and methodologies are employed in the classroom. If differentiation is seen as an end in itself, rather than as an outcome of inclusive practice, then it is inevitable that some schools/teachers will respond solely in terms of pupils' cognitive ability. The solution to this is frequently seen in terms of setting, banding or streaming by ability. For pupils who use EAL, there is an issue of equal opportunity of language access. They may well be pupils of considerable cognitive ability who need help to demonstrate mastery of concepts through the medium of English. It is unhelpful if, because of their limited command of the language, they are placed with others of lower ability. Inclusive practice should mean that the curriculum is both appropriate and motivating for all pupils and this has a role to play in sustaining positive pupil behaviour at school.

How to do it

Factors that affect the difficulty of a task include a pupil's familiarity with the materials, concepts and language used and the extent to which models, prompts and concrete referents are made available.

Differentiating learning opportunities by task, resource, support and outcome is part of inclusive classroom practice. Wherever possible, the aim should be on devising a common learning experience for all members of a class within which pupils are presented with stimuli that suit their preferred learning styles and where they have access to a range of alternative response modes. Thus, for example, a history lesson on the Great Fire of London might be presented with maps, video clips, text and pictures. A task sheet defines terms, summarises key facts and offers a choice of response modes, including: a written account (which may be structured for grammatical content); a storyboard with cartoon pictures and captions; recording a radio programme about it; or role playing how a family might have tried to save themselves.

Many of the techniques suggested by the National Literacy Strategy, such as writing frames and key word displays, as well as the Key Stage 3 language initiatives (QCA 2000b) are aimed at all learners but also allow curriculum access where language/literacy might be a barrier to learning (see also the Statement on Inclusion in the National Curriculum Handbooks (DfEE 1999a, b)).

One of the most important aims of inclusive educational practice is to help pupils take an increasingly greater responsibility for their own learning. The following matrix (Cummins 1984) is offered as a helpful way of thinking about the learning needs of different groups of pupils so that they can operate more autonomously in the classroom.

Curriculum related assessment (Cummins Framework)

What is it?

Curriculum-based assessment has advantages for bilingual pupils in that it is less discriminatory than the standardised measures of psychological tests or casual observation. However, applying the behavioural methodology of direct instruction, task analysis and precision teaching has serious disadvantages when assessing bilingual children.

In a leading publication on this subject, Jim Cummins (1984) expressed serious reservations of the model of curriculum-based assessment most commonly used by British psychologists. He pointed out several arguments against using a direct instruction approach with bilingual children. An emphasis on teacher initiation and control may actually inhibit the active involvement of the child which, linguists argue, is necessary for the development of cognitive academic language proficiency. He also argues powerfully against the reduction of meaningful context that often results from task analysis in which learning is broken down into isolated parts. One of the best ways of assisting bilingual pupils is to ensure that the knowledge or skill to be taught is embedded in a comprehensible and meaningful learning context.

The term 'curriculum related assessment' (CRA) has come to mean any method of assessing children that includes directly assessing their performance within the curriculum for the purpose of meeting their teaching needs. The Cummins Framework is offered here as one model, which can be easily used by teachers as a tool for planning and differentiating the curriculum. It can also be used as a means of recording learning outcomes by noting observations of positive achievement demonstrated in the classroom directly onto a matrix.

Why use it?

- It is simple, easy to use and understand.
- It fits with the demands of planning and differentiating in the National Curriculum.
- It considers the needs of three different groups of pupils, i.e. very able pupils, bilingual pupils and pupils with SEN.
- It should ensure that bilingual children are stretched, rather than mindlessly employed, through appropriately demanding but comprehensible tasks.
- It puts a focus on raising levels of achievement and teacher expectation through an emphasis on cognitive demand.

How to do it

- Use the two dimensions of the matrix (see p. 52) to help you consider:
  a) the particular learning styles, experience, skills and needs of individual pupils

b) the requirements of the task

c) the context and situation where the learning will take place.

- Work collaboratively with colleagues at the planning stage, especially if you share classroom and teaching responsibilities with other colleagues, bilingual assistants, nursery nurses, language or learning support staff. This will generate ideas and discussion.

- Start with one unit or aspect of a topic/programme of study you intend to teach. Start small; plot tasks and activities according to the level of cognitive demand and context embeddedness you think are involved.

- Use the worked examples on pp. 55–59 to help you get started.

- Refer to the matrix on p. 54 that gives examples of cognitive processes (but do bear in mind these are debatable and fairly meaningless when separated from their actual learning contexts).

Notes on worked examples

The examples given on the following pages have been developed at teacher workshops and are intended to get you started on the process of using the Cummins matrix as a tool for your own planning for differentiation. You will find your own solutions based on your knowledge of the learning needs of pupils in your classroom.

Key Stage 1 science (see pp. 55 and 56)

This matrix shows the possible range of pupil responses during a practical activity of 'floating and sinking' (this relates to AT1 Levels 1, 2, 3 and AT3 Levels 1, 2 and 3 of the unrevised National Curriculum science orders). This use of the matrix could be used to show pupils' evidence of learning as part of the teacher's assessment. This sort of activity is typical of those conceptual areas with which a bilingual child may be very familiar, yet not have sufficient English to demonstrate her/his mastery. The accompanying notes show some ideas for methods of recording that could be used.

Key Stage 2 geography (see pp. 57 and 58)

This example shows one teacher's attempts to plan a range of differentiated activities for a mixed Year 3 and 4 class on 'the local area' (AT Level 2). It also includes some practical ideas for materials and methodology.

Key Stage 3 English (see p. 59)

This example shows the mapping of the activities developed in a pack of materials designed to support the teaching and accessibility of a 'difficult text', Shakespeare's *Romeo and Juliet* (Field 1992). The materials were developed in collaboration with Stuart Scott and the Collaborative Learning Project (see Useful addresses), trialled in local schools and represent methodology and activities which could be adapted to any text. The pack is available with others from the Tower Hamlets Language Support Service (see Useful addresses). The use of these materials is also discussed more fully in Hall (1994).

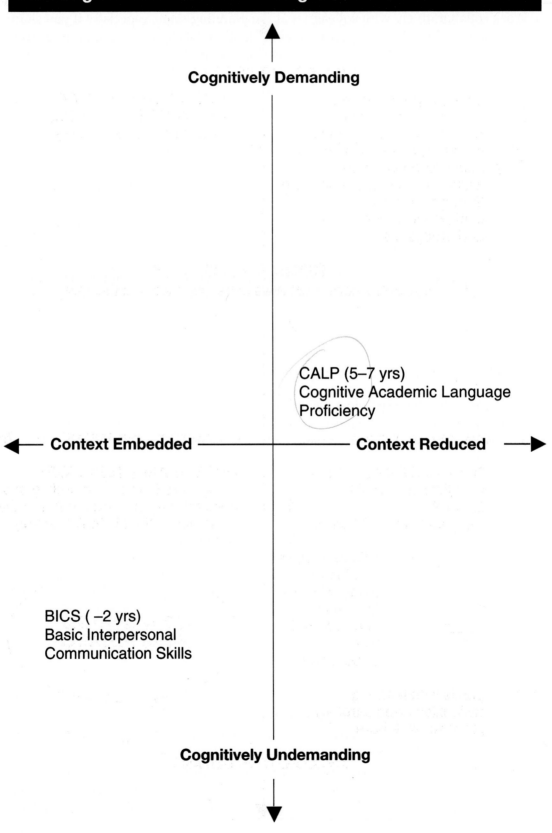

Planning for Differentiation: Using the Cummins Framework

Cognitively Demanding

CALP (5–7 yrs)
Cognitive Academic Language
Proficiency

◄── **Context Embedded** ──────── **Context Reduced** ──►

BICS (–2 yrs)
Basic Interpersonal
Communication Skills

Cognitively Undemanding

Planning for Differentiation: The Cummins Framework

HIGH COGNITIVE DEMAND

** bilingual pupils need the
majority of their work to
be set at this level so that
increasing demands are
being made on them
while ensuring understanding
through concrete and
contextual content
and processes

COGNITIVE ACADEMIC
LEARNING PROFICIENCY
(acquired in 5 to 7 years)

(bilingual pupils) ------->

** very able pupils must always be given work at this level

◄——— **CONTEXT EMBEDDED** ——————— **CONTEXT UNEMBEDDED** ———►

BASIC INTERPERSONAL
COMMUNICATION
SKILLS
(acquired within 2 years)

UNDESIRABLE TERRITORY!
if tasks are both undemanding and
abstract they are undesirable in the
classroom. What is their learning
potential?

bilingual pupils
need to move
along this axis
to ensure
achievement
with
understanding

**NO ACTIVITIES
HERE PLEASE!**

** pupils with learning
difficulties need carefully
planned work here

LOW COGNITIVE DEMAND

Cognitive Processes: Using the Cummins Framework

generalises

compares and **contrasts**

summarises

plans

classifies by known criteria

transforms, personalises given information

recalls and **reviews**

seeks solutions to problems

argues a case using evidence persuasively

identifies criteria, develops and **sustains ideas**

justifies opinion or judgement

evaluates critically

interprets evidence, makes deductions

forms hypotheses, asks further questions for investigation

predicts results

applies principles to new situation

analyses, suggests a solution and tests

COGNITIVE PROCESSES

reading to find specific information

- **identifies**

- **names**

- **matches**

- **retells**

transfers information from one medium to another

applies known procedures

describes observations

sequences

narrates with sense of beginning, middle, end

- **parrots:** repeats utterances of adult or peer

- **copies:** reproduces information from board or texts

Worked example KS1 Science: Using the Cummins Framework

Cognitively Demanding

Evidence of Learning

- makes predictions about other objects (in classroom) which might float/sink

- can state why they think objects sink or float

- sorts objects by other qualities e.g. heavy/light wood/metal

- can suggest questions/ideas based on everyday experience which can be tested

- can predict other objects (not present) which would float/sink

- can make series of related observations

- uses observations to compare expected outcome with that observed and make conclusions

◄─**Context Embedded** ── KS1 SCIENCE | AT1, L1, 2 + 3 | AT3, L1, 2, 3 | FLOATING & SINKING ── **Context Reduced**─►

- sorts objects into sets – 'these sink' – 'these float'

- water play: child states 'this sinks'; 'this floats'

> **Entry Language Skills**
>
> Pre-teach: on, under; floats sinks; object names e.g. scissors, cork etc.

Cognitively Undemanding

Floating & Sinking KS1 Science

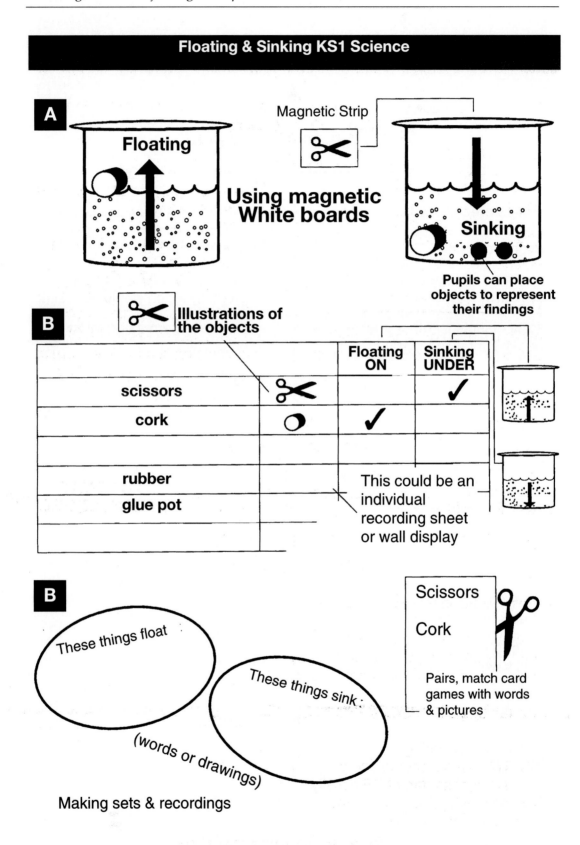

A

Floating

Magnetic Strip

Using magnetic
White boards

Sinking

Pupils can place
objects to represent
their findings

B

Illustrations of
the objects

		Floating ON	Sinking UNDER
scissors	✂		✓
cork	O	✓	
rubber			This could be an individual recording sheet or wall display
glue pot			

B

These things float

These things sink :

(words or drawings)

Making sets & recordings

Scissors

Cork

Pairs, match card
games with words
& pictures

Worked example KS2 Geography: Assessing difficult texts

HIGH COGNITIVE DEMAND

Computer: 'directions'
(Smile – The next 17)

aerial photo and map –
plot on places of interest
using colour key
(e.g. green = park)

using vocabulary bank connect
photo to name to position on map

using coordinates to describe/find
features on map

design key symbols for features –
(compare with O.S.)

design routes (treasure hunt) with
written instruction for other groups
using geographical vocabulary

GEOG KS2 — posing questions and answers about why certain features are

LOCAL AREA — AT L1, L2.

CONTEXT EMBEDDED ← → **CONTEXT UNEMBEDDED**

using aerial photo to trace routes

walking local area identifying
features matching photos and
names (and in Bengali script)

computer: 'pip' – obstacle course

'ship to shore' using
NSEW/obstacle course using
left and right as part of PE activity
in school hall/gym. (Use correct
compass point to walls!)

LOW COGNITIVE DEMAND

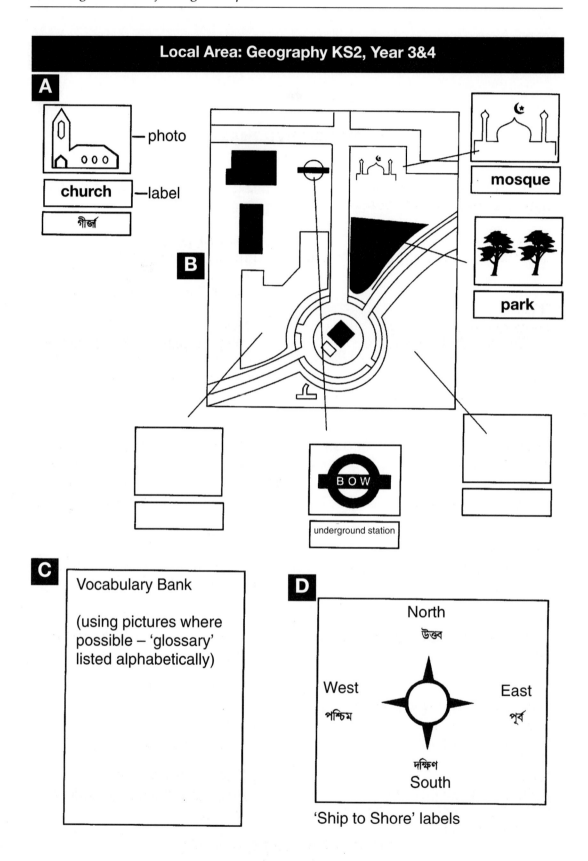

Local Area: Geography KS2, Year 3&4

A

photo

church —label

গীর্জা

B

mosque

park

B O W

underground station

C

Vocabulary Bank

(using pictures where possible – 'glossary' listed alphabetically)

D

North
উত্তর

West
পশ্চিম

East
পূর্ব

দক্ষিণ
South

'Ship to Shore' labels

Worked example KS3 English: Accessing difficult texts

HIGH COGNITIVE DEMAND

prologue
using pictorial clues to match
and sequence couplets from prologue

character
'2 minute autobiographies' using cards

text
quote quest:matching quotations to
statements about character

prologue
modern English version matched to
text

prologue
modern English version matched with
story

prologue
sequencing prologue couplets
(without clues)

character
research using blank
cards/devise quiz game using
information from text.

text
'filling the gaps' using speeches
from key scenes and full text to
research before and after

theme
'who was to blame?': prepare
debate for tribunal or discursive
essay

◄—— **CONTEXT EMBEDDED** ——————— **CONTEXT UNEMBEDDED** ——►

character
'connect four': statement about
character

story
'summary' matched with sequenced
pictures

story
'invent your own Romeo and Juliet'
sequencing pictures and telling
story from them

story
pictures and 'key words'
making posters for wall display
using key words

Romeo and Juliet
ENGLISH K.S.3

TEXTS to be made available
to pupils:

● standard school text
*abbreviated text
*prose version
*abbreviated prose text

(*Leon Garfield texts)
Animated Shakespeare films
also useful

LOW COGNITIVE DEMAND

7 School systems

School responsibilities

Clearly, the management and administration of a school has a key role to play in ensuring the greatest possible progress of all its pupils. It is sometimes said that the success or failure of a school stands or falls by the quality of its leadership and the effectiveness of the systems in place. They are the responsibility of senior management but are often delegated to senior teachers or heads of department/faculty. Good systems will withstand staff changes as they are not dependent on one charismatic individual. To be fully effective, they need to be realistic, practical and manageable, clearly understood, owned and used by all staff. These should form part of the whole-school policy on assessment reporting and recording as it is the systems that are responsible for putting the parts of the policy into everyday practice.

Whatever separate procedures are used for the assessment of bilingual or SEN pupils, they need to relate to National Curriculum criteria. OFSTED teams are asked to judge schools largely on the standards of achievement and the quality of teaching and learning. A survey (OFSTED 1994b) that looked at educational support for minority ethnic communities has reported that the most successful assessment practices 'made effective use of comprehensive records to which all staff contributed, to raise the achievement of the pupils in National Curriculum terms'. It concludes, 'The best assessment recording and reporting procedures showed the pupil's attainment in National Curriculum terms and used the language stages to give a baseline from which to judge progress'.

SEN: Revised Draft Code of Practice

The Revised Draft Code of Practice on the Identification and Assessment of Special Educational Needs (DfEE 2000a) gives guidance on the 'discharge of functions' under Part IV of the 1996 Education Act (DfEE 1996) for those pupils who fail to learn and progress within the general arrangements of the school. The Revised Draft Code simplifies the 1994 five-stage Code into new stages characterised as follows:

- **School Action:** the SENCO takes lead responsibility for gathering information and for coordinating the child's SEN provision, working with the child's teachers. An Individual Education Plan (IEP) is written and reviewed.

- **School Action Plus:** teachers and the SENCO are supported by specialists from outside the school by the LEA and/or other outside agencies.
- **Statutory Assessment:** the LEA considers the need for statutory assessment and, if appropriate, makes a multi-disciplinary assessment.
- **Statement of Special Educational Needs:** the LEA considers the need for a statement of SEN and, if appropriate, makes a statement and arranges, monitors and reviews provision.

The demands and implications of the Code mean that the school's SENCO will have a key role in creating workable systems for the regular assessment, review and monitoring of those pupils registered. SENCOs are also responsible for liaising with parents, agencies and support services. It is suggested that about 20 per cent of pupils may have SEN and that only about 2 per cent (nationally) are likely to have needs of sufficient severity to warrant statutory statements or special school places. As they will have considerable responsibility under the Revised Draft Code of Practice for monitoring at least 18 per cent of the pupils on role, it is to be hoped that SENCOs will now be given a status commensurate with other senior members of staff in recognition of the additional work and responsibility required.

Bilingual pupils' representation on the Revised Draft Code of Practice stages

In Chapter 1, it was stated that schools should bear in mind the figures given above when checking the balance between bilingual pupils and those with SEN. As a rough guide, the percentage of the bilingual pupil population should be reflected as a ratio of the school's registered SEN pupils. For example, take the case of a non-selective secondary school of 1,000 pupils which has a bilingual population of 40 per cent, i.e. 400 bilingual pupils. They could expect under the law of averages to have a total of about 200 pupils registered across the SEN stages. Of these 200 they might expect 80 of these pupils (40 per cent of the 200) to be bilingual.

This is a simple and fairly crude measurement, but it will help in making a judgement about whether too great a proportion or too few of your bilingual pupils are perceived as having SEN. It is a way of checking your school's understanding that, although the difficulties of language access of some bilingual children must not be confused with learning difficulties, some bilingual children (approximately 20 per cent) are equally likely to need to be registered as having SEN.

Of course there are all sorts of local variations – these national average figures serve only as a guide. In some schools and areas, social conditions will create higher incidences of SEN than the national average. Bilingual children also come from a wide variety of backgrounds but, except in instances where research has proven that certain physical health/sensory disabilities are more prevalent, there is nothing to suggest that children from ethnic minority communities should be either under- or over-represented in school populations as children with SEN.

LEAs and SEN audit systems

Many LEAs are presently considering the introduction of a system of audit for SEN within their area. This is a funding issue and has arisen partly in response to Audit Commission reports on SEN and the rise in the numbers of pupils nationally who are being statemented. The statutory nature of these statements of SEN (roughly 2 per cent of all children) require considerable financial resourcing. This has meant that less money is available to the majority of pupils with SEN in schools without statements (18 per cent). Because of associated cuts in centrally provided services, it has been increasingly perceived by parents and teachers that statementing is the only way to ensure that extra resources will be available to meet a child's needs. LEAs and schools are looking for a more equitable method of ensuring support in mainstream schools for pupils without recourse to statutory assessment.

Some LEAs, such as Kent and Northampton, have devised and run a system of SEN audit which they have tested and revised in the light of experience. This devolves to schools the accountability for the identification of pupils prior to statementing and the responsibility for the interventions made. Other LEAs are using these models on which to base their own. Central government argues that schools already have additional funding for factors in addition to age-weighted pupil units (APUs), usually based on proxy indicators such as numbers of pupils entitled to free school meals and other socio-economic factors. The Revised Draft Code of Practice is therefore described as a 'nil resources' initiative! It is felt that with greater financial accountability and the delegation of budgets directly to schools, the significance of the publication of the government's Revised Draft Code of Practice may well be a catalyst for further action. There is also a feeling in some quarters that, because of central government's close interest in systems of audit, they may be imposed on those LEAs who have not got their 'Acts' (*sic!*) together. Head teachers now have a considerable say in whether parts of the education budget are held for centrally organised services or delegated directly to schools. Therefore it is critical that there is agreement and moderation between schools so that funding for pupils at various stages of SEN registers is seen to be equitable and is used for the intended purpose. An audit system also means that schools and authorities are much more publicly accountable for expenditure on those children whom the money is intended to support.

Bilingual pupils presently represent over 60 per cent of the school population overall in Tower Hamlets. In the borough, a working group, which included head teachers, attempted to write descriptors of pupils at the school-based stages of SEN as a proposal for an audit to be considered by local head teachers. Issues of support for bilingual pupils were directly addressed and written in. There are obviously dangers in doing this and it is an issue that has not, until recently, been directly addressed elsewhere – probably because it is so contentious. The descriptors obviously fit local conditions and current levels of provision in Tower Hamlets. The accompanying notes on bilingual pupils were distributed to schools for their considerations in rewriting SEN policy documents where issues concerning bilingual pupils must be addressed in operating the Revised Draft Code of Practice proposals. The audit was written with descriptors fitting across the requirements of the Code to prevent a situation where two separate systems of assessing SEN pupils might be required from schools (they have been somewhat updated by the editors of this second edition in order to reflect the proposed stages of the revised Code).

It is expected that local schools will have very clear guidelines for the expected progress in the acquisition of English at early language levels. If pupils continue to cause concern, and there is clear evidence of their lack of progress after additional support and help with English has been given over a reasonable period of time and their progress closely monitored, then they may need to be identified and registered for SEN at the School Action stage.

Bilingual pupils on SEN registers (notes for guidance)

School Action: assessment

- It is expected that language support will continue and will contribute to a fuller picture of the biligual child's acquisition of, and learning in, English.
- Some assessment of first language will be helpful as this will help to clarify whether there is a delay or difficulty that is also apparent in the first language.
- Sight and hearing checks are particularly important at this stage to children learning in a second language, especially if the pupil is a recent arrival or refugee, as sensory loss cannot be assumed to have been identified at an earlier point.

Curricular needs

- Even if pupils are registered for SEN, continued language support and assessment will be required. Pupils should still be targeted and included for group support within the classroom.
- The additional help from the class teacher or other adults should include input from a language support teacher to suggest methodology, group activities, materials and contextual referents appropriate to support the child's learning in class. This support may also be given by the bilingual instructor/assistant for some of the time.
- Peer support in a group which includes other home language speakers is desirable, but it is also important to ensure that the group includes more fluent English-speaking peers.
- In addition to the language support provided in class, targeted and specific language and learning support may be appropriate for some bilingual pupils at School Action stage.

Equipment/materials

- Bilingual pupils may require increased access to shared equipment and differentiated materials including bilingual or translated texts.
- Information technology (IT) based support is very fruitful in terms of multisensory and culturally appropriate materials. Some excellent programs are available that allow children to interact in a variety of ways not totally dependent on the written text.

Access to agencies

- Pupils may need access to local resources of advice/support in the community. If school staff or home and community contacts cannot be provided in a minority language then translation/interpretation services may be appropriate.

  NB *Schools may need advice and/or INSET on the early identification of bilingual pupils with SEN.*

School Action Plus: assessment

As for School Action with the addition of:

- An advisory teacher may be involved in assessing difficulties or in contributing to an IEP at this stage.
- This may involve the expertise in assessment skills from a member of staff. This could be done by a monolingual teacher with these skills working alongside a bilingual member of staff with an understanding of SEN.

Curricular needs

- In addition to the language support provided in class, targeted and specific language support may be appropriate for some bilingual pupils at School Action Plus.
- Support to address specific curricular objectives could be provided by a language support teacher or bilingual instructor. This must then be clearly specified on the IEP and should be additional to any other targeted curriculum support provided for learning or other difficulties.

Access to agencies

- Some areas may have local community or bilingual services which can be helpful at this point. Check the local situation.
- A bilingual speech and language assessment may also be appropriate.
- A first language assessment of expressive/receptive language would give valuable further information. Some assessment of conceptual development through first language would also provide significant additional evidence.

8 Conclusions

It is to be hoped that the wide range of ideas and descriptions of various aspects of assessment in this book will help individuals and schools see more clearly that although language and learning difficulties should not be confused, some bilingual pupils are likely to have SEN. Teachers need to trust and rely on their own professional skills and abilities to assess the competence of bilingual pupils in collaboration with colleagues. Schools need to establish good policies and reliable systems for recording and reporting to ensure that pupils are neither overlooked nor wrongly assigned.

The key to accurate and well-considered assessment decisions about children whose learning is causing concern is the quality of the consideration in the search for information and evidence. The solutions are often to be found within the mainstream mixed-ability classroom, where the education of bilingual pupils and those who may have SEN is a part of every teacher's job. The assessment of pupils' needs is increasingly likely to rely on teachers' observation and evidence rather than on a formal testing of cognitive processing alone. Equally, there is less likelihood that factors will be seen as deficits within the child, separate somehow from an evaluation of the adequacy and appropriateness of classroom methodology and materials. In the same way as language and learning are inextricably linked, so there is an undoubted relationship between self-esteem, behaviour and learning.

That the good classroom practice of skilled and experienced teachers can support the learning and achievement of bilingual pupils in school is in abundant evidence in many schools. Hopefully the ideas developed in this book will renew your faith in your own skills and good practice, and encourage you and your colleagues to develop this important aspect of your work.

Useful addresses

- The **Collaborative Learning Project** is run by Stuart Scott as a 'swapshop' for teachers' materials developed from collaborative and group work in classrooms. To join you send in your materials. A catalogue of materials for sale at photocopied rates is available. Stuart is available to run workshops on using/developing collaborative games and activities in the classroom and is also doing a lot of work with European countries (see also Intercultural Education Partnership below). Contact:

  Stuart Scott
  17 Barford Street
  London N1 0QB
  Tel: 020 7226 8885

- The **Intercultural Education Partnership** has been supported by the Commission of the European Union and the United Kingdom Departments for Education. It offers various projects as a forum for issues of common interest with European counterparts in the teaching of bilingual/ethnic minority children. Up-to-date information is available from:

  Mandy Slattery
  17 Barford Street
  London N1 0QB
  Tel: 020 7226 8885
  Fax: 020 7704 1350
  Website: www.atschool.eduweb.co.uk/collearn/index.hgml

- **National Association of Language Development in the Curriculum (NALDIC)** is a network for UK teachers 'working for pupils with English as an additional language'. For membership and publications, contact:

  NALDIC
  c/o EMA South Area Centre
  Tolpits Lane, Watford
  Herts WD18 6LP
  Tel: 01923 248584
  Fax: 01923 225130

- **National Association for Special Educational Needs (NASEN)** publishes two excellent journals with articles on various aspects of SEN: *Support for Learning* and the *British Journal of Special Education*. It also provides a national forum for discussion and debate through local associations and sponsors special needs education exhibitions and seminars. Contact NASEN at:

NASEN House
4/5 Amber Business Village
Amber Close
Amington, Tamworth, Staffs
B77 4RP
Tel: 01827 311500
Fax: 01827 313005
Email: welcome@nasen.org.uk
Website: http//www.nasen.org.uk

- **Tower Hamlets Language Support Service** distributes the books marked ** in the references. A catalogue is also available of materials such as tapes, story props and packs. Packs for the teaching of Bengali as a modern foreign language at GCSE are also available. Contact:

Tower Hamlets Language Support Service
Professional Development Centre
English Street
London E3 4TA
Tel: 020 7364 6350
Website: www.towerhamlets.pdc.org.uk

- The **ESL/SEN Network at SENJIT** is a useful forum for teachers in London and the South East which organises termly talks/workshops on various areas of interest. Information and contacts via:

Nick Peacey
SENJIT Institute of Education, University of London
20 Bedford Way
London WC1H 0AL
Tel: 020 7612 6273
Website: www.ioe.ac.uk

- The **British Dyslexia Association (BDA)** is a national organisation promoting awareness of and interventions to support people with specific learning difficulties (dyslexia). They produce numerous publications and journals as well as validating the training of specialist teachers. Contact:

British Dyslexia Association
98 London Road
Reading RG1 5AU
Tel: Helpline 0118 966 8271 Admin 0118 966 2677
Email: info@dyslexiahelp-bda.demon.co.uk
Website: http//www.bda-dyslexia.org.uk/

Useful resources

ICT resources

Clicker 4: Crick Software. www. cricksoft.com
Wordbar: Crick Software. www. clickergrids.com
Tel: (01604) 671691
Writing with Symbols: Widget Software.
Starspell 2000.
Inspiration: (A tool to develop ideas and organise thinking). Inspiration Software Inc. www.inspiration.com. UK distributors: Tag Developments.
Hyperstudio: (A simple multimedia authoring program). Roger Wagner Publishing Inc. UK distributors: Tag Developments
'mimio' (whiteboard board attachment converts any whiteboard to interactive resource). Virtual Ink.

Websites (described in their own words)

DfEE: National Grid for Learning Inclusion
A catalogue of resources to support individual learning needs.
www.inclusion.ngfl.gov.uk

DfEE: The Standards Site
Disseminating practical guidance and examples of good practice in schools in England.
www.standards.dfee.gov.uk

BECTA Inclusion Websit (British Educational Communications and Technology Agency)
Best site of many sites dealing with ICT and how it can support many learners.
www.becta.org.uk/inclusion/index.htm

VTC Conferencing Websites
Include discussion forums for a variety of SEN/EAL/inclusion professionals
http://forum.ngfl.gov.uk/cgi-bin/webx?vtc

DfEE SEN
A wide range of advice and materials for teachers, parents and other working with children with SEN.
www.sen.dfee.gov.uk

Appendices

Photocopiable forms/slides for INSET

IDENTIFICATION AND ASSESSMENT
Bilingual Learners

■ **BASIC INFORMATION**
About the Child at Home
and in the Community

■ **SCREENING**
Physical/Medical/Sensory

■ **HYPOTHESIS TESTING**
Consideration

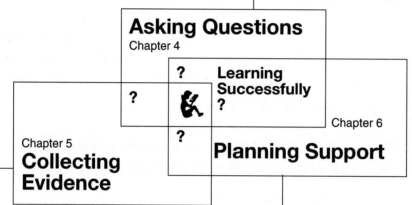

Asking Questions
Chapter 4

? **Learning Successfully?**
?

Chapter 6

Chapter 5
Collecting Evidence

Planning Support

■ **LANGUAGE LEVEL**
Stages of English
EMAG and Records

■ **FIRST LANGUAGE
DEVELOPMENT INFORMATION?**

■ **READING STRATEGIES**
Scales/Recovery (Chapter 5)
Miscue Analysis

■ **SAMPLES OF WORK**
Pupil self-assessment
School records/assessment AR & R

■ **NATIONAL CURRICULUM
ATTAINMENT**

■ **INDIVIDUAL ACTION PLAN**

■ **DIFFERENTIATION**

■ **CURRICULUM RELATED ASSESSMENT
(Cummins Matrix)**
Curriculum Planning

■ **SCHOOLS SYSTEM OF SUPPORT**
(Chapter 7)

BILINGUAL CHILDREN
WHAT THE RESEARCH TELLS US

- Children take up to two years to develop 'basic interpersonal communication skills' (playground/street survival language) BUT it takes much longer, perhaps from five to seven years or more, to acquire the full range of literacy skills ('cognitive academic language proficiency') needed to cope with the literacy demands of GCSE.

- A silent (receptive) period is natural for some pupils when learning a second language and not a sign of learning difficulties in the first/early stages.

- There are developmental factors in common to both native and second language acquisition. For more information, refer to Cummings (1996) and the 'dual iceberg' theory.

- Teachers/schools should have basic information available about the language backgrounds of bilingual pupils (see Chapter 4).

- There should be an awareness by all that a focus on the first language is a valuable channel to support learning and NOT a hindrance. Teachers should not advocate the use of English only, either at school or at home.

- Parents should be encouraged to share language and literacy in speaking and listening as well as in reading and writing. This can be as valuable in first/home language as in English.

- Bilingualism can be educationally enriching and has a positive effect on intellectual performance.

- Bilingualism should be valued as a special achievement.

- Where there are academic difficulties, teachers should first critically examine the teaching they are offering in terms of motivation and the language used.

The Bilingual Pupil at Home and in the Community

Basic Family Details

Full Name .... D.O.B. ....

Name child is called at home .... Age Now ....

Name to be called at school (if different) ....

Arrival date in UK (if not British born) ....

Length of previous schooling abroad ....

Names of schools/LEAs in UK ....

Number of terms of UK schooling...

Date of long extended absences from schooling ....

Place of birth ....

Religion ....

Does child live with both parents as part of family unit? ....

Festivals observed ....

If not who are carers? ....

Mothers name..

Dietary needs ....

Fathers name ....

(School correspondence should be addressed to ....

Most useful written language for family is...

Names and ages of siblings ....

....

....

Languages

Languages spoken at home by pupils to ....

Mother... Grandparents ....

Father .... Siblings ....

Languages used by family members to child ....

Can child read/write languages other than English?...

write .... read ....

Is child learning to read/write in languages other than English?..........................

....

Community Links

Does child attend any school/class in community/ ....

Mother tongue class .... community school ....

religious .... Mosque/classes ....

What languages are used taught there?...

What is the name/address of organisation? ....

....

....

Who is contact person for group?...

Is interpreter needed for teacher to communicate with parents? ....

If so, who might this be? ....

Family view of important illnesses/or other medical factors seen as important ......

....

Is child right handed? left handed?...

Should child be using glasses hearing aid/other aids for learning? ....

....

Does child require any regular medication during school day ....

....

Secondary pupil languages form

What languages do I use?

What languages do they use to me?

ME

Mother

Father

Sisters & Brothers

Grandparents

Languages used by ....

I think that I talk .... a bit   quite well   very well

I read .... a bit   quite well   very well

I can copy ....

I write it   a bit   quite well   very well

When I think about home, I think in ....

When I am at school, I think in ....

Can I say all I want to in ....?   Yes   No

Can I say all I want to in English ....?   Yes   No

I think I am best at using the .... language, at present

Date completed ....

Planning for Differentiation: The Cummins Framework

Bibliography

Ayers, H., Clarke, D., Ross, A. and Bonathan, M. (1993) *Assessing Individual Needs*. London: David Fulton Publishers.

Barrs, M., Ellis, S., Hester, H. and Kelly, A. V. (1988) *The Primary Language Record Handbook*. London: Centre for Language in Primary Education (CLPE).

Barrs, M., Ellis, S., Hester, H. and Thomas, A. (1990) *Patterns of Learning*. London: Centre for Language in Primary Education (CLPE).

Barthorpe, T. and Visser, J. (1989) *Differentiation: Your Responsibility*. Stafford: National Association for Special Educational Needs (NASEN).

Bennett, N. and Barnes, D. (1992) *Managing Classroom Groups*. London: Simon & Schuster.

Blackledge, A. (ed.) (1994) *Teaching Bilingual Children*. Stoke-on-Trent: Trentham Books.

Bourne, J. and McPake, J. (1991) *Partnership Teaching*. London: National Foundation for Educational Research (NFER)/Department of Education and Science (DES) for HMSO.

Brent Language Service (1999) *Enriching Literacy – Text, Talk and Tales in Today's Classroom*. Stoke-on-Trent: Trentham Books.

Buxton, C. (1994) *Language Activities for Bilingual Learners*. London: Tower Hamlets Language Support Service.

Cinamon, D. and Gravelle, M. (1988) 'Bilingualism is NOT a learning difficulty', *Gnosis* 12.

Clay, M. (1979) *The Early Detection of Reading Difficulties*. London: Heinemann.

Cline, T. (1998) 'The assessment of special educational needs for bilingual children', *British Journal of Special Education* **25**, 4.

Cline, T. and Frederickson, N. (1991) *Bilingual Pupils and the National Curriculum: Overcoming Difficulties in Teaching and Learning*. London: University College London.

Cline, T. and Frederickson, N. (eds) (1994) *Progress in Curriculum Related Assessment for Bilingual Pupils*. Clevedon: Multilingual Matters.

Cline, T and Frederickson, N. (1996) *Curriculum Related Assessment, Cummins and Bilingual Children*. Clevedon: Multilingual Matters.

Cline, T. and Frederickson, N. (1999) 'Identification and Assessment of Dyslexia in Bi/multilingual Pupils', *International Journal of Bilingual Education and Bilingualism* **12**, 81–93.

Commission for Racial Equality (CRE) (1986) *The Teaching of English as a Second Language: The Report of a Formal Enquiry in Calderdale LEA.* London: CRE.

Commission for Racial Equality (CRE) (2000) *Learning for All: Standards for Racial Equality in Schools.* London: CRE.

Cummins, J. (1984) *Bilingualism and Special Education: Issues in Assessment and Pedagogy.* Clevedon: Multilingual Matters.

Cummins, J. (1996) *Negotiating Identities: Education for Empowerment in a Diverse Society.* Ontario, Calif.: California Association for Bilingual Education (CABE) (Distributed in UK by Trentham Books, Stoke-on-Trent.)

Department for Education (DfE) (1993) *Education Act 1993.* London: HMSO.

Department for Education (DfE) (1994) *Code of Practice on the Identification and Assessment of Special Educational Needs.* London: DfE.

Department for Education and Employment (DfEE) (1996) *Education Act 1996.* London: HMSO.

Department for Education and Employment (DfEE) (1999a) *The National Curriculum Handbook for Primary School Teachers.* London: DfEE/Qualifications and Curriculum Authority (QCA).

Department for Education and Employment (DfEE) (1999b) *The National Curriculum Handbook for Secondary Teachers.* London: DfEE/Qualifications and Curriculum Authority (QCA).

Department for Education and Employment (DfEE) (1999c) *From Exclusion to Inclusion.* London: DfEE.

Department for Education and Employment (DfEE) (2000a) *The Revised Draft Code of Practice on the Identification and Assessment of Special Educational Needs.* London: DfEE.

Department for Education and Employment (DfEE) (2000b) *Removing the Barriers, Raising Achievement Levels for Minority Ethnic Pupils.* London: DfEE.

Department of Education and Science (DES) (1981) *Education Act 1981.* London: HMSO.

Department of Education and Science (DES) (1985) *Education for All: The Report of the Committee of Enquiry into the Education of Children from Ethnic Minorities* (The Swann Report). London: HMSO.

Desforges, M. and Kerr, T. (1984) 'Developing Bilingual Children's English in School', *Educational and Child Psychology* **1**(1).

Dulay, H. and Burt, M. (1974) 'Natural Sequences in Second Language Acquisition', Language Learning **24.**

Dulay, H., Burt, M. and Krashen, S. (1982) *Language Two.* Oxford: Oxford University Press.

Duncan, D. (ed.) (1989) *Working with Bilingual Language Disability.* London and New York: Chapman & Hall.

Field, C. (1992) *Collaborative Learning Project: Romeo and Juliet.* London: Tower Hamlets Language Support Service.

Fisher, R. (1995a) *Teaching Children to Learn.* Cheltenham: Stanley Thornes.

Fisher, R. (1995b) *Teaching Children to Think.* Cheltenham: Stanley Thornes.

Gardner, H. (1993) *Frames of Mind: The Theory of Multiple Intelligences.* London: Fontana.

Goodman, K. S. (1973) 'Psycholinguistic universals in the reading process', in Smith, F. (ed.) *Psycholinguistics and Reading*. New York: Holt, Rhinehart & Winston.

Graf, V. (1992) 'Minimising the Inappropriate Referral and Placement of Ethnic Minority Students in Special Education', in Cline, T. (ed.) *The Assessment of Special Educational Needs: International Perspectives*. London: Routledge.

Gravelle, M. (2000) *Planning for Bilingual Learners, an Inclusive Curriculum*. Stoke-on-Trent: Trentham Books.

Hall, D. (1994)' Differentiating the Secondary Curriculum', in Cline, T. and Frederickson, N. (eds) *Progress in Curriculum Related Assessment for Bilingual Pupils*. Clevedon: Multilingual Matters.

Hart, S. (2000) *Thinking Through Teaching*. London: David Fulton Publishers.

Keel, P. (ed.) (1994) *Assessment in the Multi-ethnic Primary Classroom*. Stoke-on-Trent: Trentham Books.

Kerr, T. and Desforges, M. (1988) 'Developing Bilingual Children's English in School', in Verma, G. and Pumfrey, P. (eds) *Educational Attainments: Issues and Outcomes in Multicultural Education*. London: Falmer Press.

Krashen, S. (1981*) Second Language Acquisition and Second Language Learning*. Oxford: Pergamon Press.

Lohman, D., Hagen, E. and Thorndyke, R. (2001) *NFER Cognitive Abilities Tests*. Windsor: National Foundation for Educational Research.

Mattes, L. and Omark, D. (1984) *Speech and Language Assessment for the Bilingual Handicapped*. San Diego, CA: College Hill Press.

McWilliam, N. (1998) *What's in a Word?* Stoke-on-Trent: Trentham Books.

Miller, N. (ed.) (1984) *Bilingualism and Language Disability: Assessment and Remediation*. San Diego, CA: College Hill Press.

Mills, R. W. and Mills, J. (1993) *Bilingualism in the Primary School*. London: Routledge.

National Association for Language Development in the Curriculum (NALDIC) (1999) Working Paper 5: The Distinctiveness of English as an Additional Language. Hounslow: NALDIC.

National Oracy Project (1993) *Learning Together Through Talk KS1 & 2* (ed. G. Baddeley) and *Learning Together Through Talk KS3 &4* (ed. H. Kemeny). London: Hodder & Stoughton.

Office for Standards in Education (OFSTED) (1994a) *Handbook for the Inspection of Schools*. London: HMSO.

Office for Standards in Education (OFSTED) (1994b) *Educational Support for Minority Ethnic Communities: A survey of educational provision funded under Section 11 of the 1966 Local Government Act*. London: OFSTED.

Office for Standards in Education (OFSTED) (1999) *Raising the Attainment of Minority Ethnic Pupils: School and LEA Response*. London: OFSTED.

Qualifications and Curriculum Authority (QCA) (2000a) *A Language in Common*. Sudbury: QCA.

Qualifications and Curriculum Authority (QCA) (2000b) *Language for Learning in Key Stage 3*. Sudbury: QCA.

Raven, J., Raven, J. C. and Court, J. H. (1998) *Raven's Standard Progressive Matrices*. Oxford: Psychology Press.

Reid, J., Forrestal, P. and Cook, J. (1989) *Small Group Learning in the Classroom*. Chalk Face Press.

Riding, R. and Rayner, S. (1998) *Cognitive Styles and Learning Strategies: Understanding Style Differences in Learning Behaviour.* London: David Fulton Publishers.

Robson, A. (1986) 'Bilingual learners-school based assessment', *Gnosis* 10.

Robson, A. (1991) 'Differentiation for Bilingual Pupils in the National Curriculum' in Cline, T. and Frederickson, N. (eds) *Bilingual Pupils and the National Curriculum.* London: University College London.

Shah, S. (1990) 'Assessment by monolingual teachers of developing bilinguals at Key Stage 1', *Multicultural Teaching* **9**(1).

Shell, R. (1992) *Language Works.* Tower Hamlets Learning by Design Block C. London: Tower Hamlets Language Support Service.

Shell, R. (1997) Language Works 2. London: Tower Hamlets Language Support Service.

Skutnabb-Kangas, T. (1981) *Bilingualism or Not: From Shame to Struggle.* Clevedon: Multilingual Matters.

Sunderland, H., Klein, C., Savinson, R. and Partridge, T. (1997) *Dyslexia and the Bilingual Learner.* London: Language and Literacy Unit.

Tomlinson, S. (1982) *A Sociology of Special Education.* London: Routledge & Kegan Paul.

Visser, J. (1993) *Differentiation: Making it work.* Stafford: National Association for Special Educational Needs (NASEN).

Wray, D. and Lewis, M. (1997) *Extending Literacy: Children reading and writing non-fiction.* London: Routledge.

Wright, A. (1991) 'The Assessment of Bilingual Pupils with Reported Learning Difficulties', in Cline, T. and Frederickson, N. *Bilingual Pupils and the National Curriculum.* London: University College London.

Index